Dilemmas in Teaching English to Speakers of Other Languages

40 CASES

Dilemmas in Teaching English to Speakers of Other Languages

40 CASES

Dorothy S. Messerschmitt
and Johnnie Johnson Hafernik

Ann Arbor
THE UNIVERSITY OF MICHIGAN PRESS

ISBN-13: 978-0-472-03378-2

2012   2011   2010   2009   4   3   2   1

Dedication

To a dear friend, Constance O'Keefe

ACKNOWLEDGMENTS

The idea for this book grew out of our experiences. Making the book a reality was the result of collective endeavors and the involvement of many colleagues and friends. We owe a debt of gratitude to each person who has helped us along the way. First, we thank our students and colleagues at the University of San Francisco and other colleagues and friends who shared their stories, experiences, and insights. We especially thank Dennis Bacigalupi, Mari McDermott, Bernadette Pedagno, Trish Pashby, Constance O'Keefe, and Gloria Yee for their support, conversations, and insights about situations and issues presented in this book. Bernadette Pedagno and Constance O'Keefe read earlier portions of the manuscript and provided valuable feedback and suggestions, which we appreciate. We extend a special thanks to our colleague, Stephanie Vandrick, for her generosity, critiques of drafts, and unwavering support in us and in the project.

We also thank two University of Michigan Press anonymous reviewers whose thoughtful comments pushed us to rethink and revise our manuscript in ways that made the book stronger. Our thanks also go to Kelly Sippell of the University of Michigan Press for her belief in the project and her guidance throughout the process. Finally, for their patience and loving support, we thank our husbands—David Messerschmitt and John E. Hafernik—and our daughters—Laura Messerschmitt and Carolyn Hafernik.

—D. S. M.
—J. J. H.

CONTENTS

INTRODUCTION AND HOW TO USE THIS BOOK

——————————————————— Because teaching English to speakers of other languages (TESOL) is an exciting and complex challenge, the realities of the classroom reach far beyond what can be presented in a typical teacher education program. Several years ago, we began noticing and discussing common situations and dilemmas that arise in the post-secondary ESOL classroom. We especially became interested in those issues that do not involve linguistic knowledge (i.e., phonology, morphology, syntax, semantics, or pragmatics) or other content typically covered in teacher education programs like pedagogy, basic classroom management, testing, or use of technology. We became interested in issues that go beyond the curriculum and, in contrast, are seldom presented systematically or in much depth in teacher education classes. Nonetheless, these issues affect instructors and their classrooms on a daily basis. How instructors handle them affects their success and effectiveness as educators and contributes to their feelings of self-worth.

The types of issues we are referring to are situations such as when a student gives a teacher a gift or asks for permission to submit a paper late or where a student exhibits suicidal behavior. These dilemmas are not limited to student-instructor interactions but include all the interactions among faculty, students, and administrators, both inside and outside the classroom. Colleagues and former students tell us of situations they were unprepared for and surprised by, dilemmas that they grappled with on an emotional and intellectual level.

Once we began noticing such dilemmas, we were surprised by their frequency and variety. In a given week, an instructor might be confronted with several dilemmas, some that had to be dealt with immediately and others that could be reflected on and discussed with colleagues and confidantes. This book features cases that confront ethical issues, a subject prevalent today in society and in education (e.g., Ethical Standards of the American Educational Research Association [AERA], 1992; Hafernik, Messerschmitt, & Vandrick, 2002; Johnston, 2003; NAFSA Code of Ethics, 1989; National Educators

Association [NEA] Code of Ethics, 1975). In this textbook, we view ethics and ethical practice broadly and do not confine it to codes of behavior; instead we link it to pedagogy, belief systems, and how members of a community treat each other. Although not interchangeable, other terms commonly used include *values* and *morals.*

In this book, we adopt Cohen's (2003) understanding of "right conduct" and his approach to ethics as problem solving. Cohen argues that "one way to understand right conduct is to imagine it on a continuum of etiquette-ethics-politics" (p. 20). He argues that the difference in each is a matter of scale, "that etiquette is small-scale ethics" (p. 48). Viewing ethics as problem solving, Cohen outlines his set of principles that he holds profoundly moral and upon which he operates.

> These values include honesty, kindness, compassion, generosity and fair-
> ness. I embrace actions that will increase the supply of human happiness,
> that will not contribute to human suffering, that are concordant with
> an egalitarian society, that will augment individual freedom, particularly
> freedom of thought and expression. (p. 10)

Cohen contends that all these values must be considered and that deciding upon a course of action requires "diplomacy among the competing principles" (p. 10).

Other cases included do not have a clear ethical dimension. However, even those that can be identified as non-ethical in nature tend to speak to social responsibility, professionalism, and humanity. Thus, cases allude to ethical aspects of issues throughout the book.

Our interest in these dilemmas and the issues they raise has continued to grow, along with our interest in how faculty members decide to address and respond to these situations. We also believe that faculty self-examination, reflection, and discussion of such dilemmas can help when issues do arise and, thus, can lead to reasoned and thoughtful action. Indeed, this is the premise on which we have based the book.

This book is an outgrowth of our interest in these often overlooked situations. It is meant to help novice, less experienced, and experienced faculty better understand their own values as well as the perspectives of others, within the context of the post-secondary and adult ESOL classroom in the United States.

Reflection Matters

The concept of reflection is central to this book: reflection on situations used as examples, on contexts, on diverse perspectives, on one's belief system, and on one's social responsibilities. Dewey (1910) defines *reflective thinking* as

> always more or less troublesome because it involves overcoming the inertia that inclines one to accept suggestions at their face value; it involves willingness to endure a condition of mental unrest and disturbance. Reflective thinking, in short, means judgment suspended during further inquiry; and suspense is likely to be somewhat painful. . . . To maintain the state of doubt and to carry on systematic and protracted inquiry—these are the essentials of thinking. (p. 13)

Dewey makes a distinction between action that is routine and action that is reflective, stating that reflective action "involves active, persistent and careful consideration of any belief or practice in light of the reasons that support it and the further consequences to which it leads" (cited in Zeichner & Liston, 1996, p. 9). He stresses the need for balance between routine action and thought and action (i.e., reflection). Integral to reflective action are three attitudes: (1) open mindedness—willingness to listen carefully and accept weaknesses of one's own and others' perspectives; (2) responsibility—careful consideration of the personal, academic, and social and political consequences of an action; and (3) wholeheartedness—willingness to examine one's own assumptions and beliefs and to approach all situations as learning situations (Dewey, cited in Zeichner & Liston, 1996, pp. 10–11).

Schön (1983) argues that reflective teaching helps individuals think about and make more conscious tacit knowledge; in this process, they can examine, criticize, and improve their knowledge and practice. He also stresses the importance for reflective educators to "frame and reframe problems in light of information gained from the settings in which they work" (p. 16). The disposition to reinterpret and reframe problems and experiences, Schön says, is an almost Zen-like "mindfulness" (p. 17). In fact, in Tremmel's classic article (1993) "Zen and the Art of Reflective Practice," he discusses Schön's idea of "reflection-in-action," with its emphasis on the present moment and the Zen concept of mindfulness, paying attention, and being in the present. Tremmel argues that paying attention is an important element in mindfulness and in reflective teaching. Tremmel notes that "Schön's notion of action focuses attention on the artistry of the practitioner in the present moment, simultaneously doing and learning and coming to know" (p. 438). This creates a paradox in that there are no solutions or certain methods, so "the paradox is that of the practitioner acting as if she knew, but being willing not to know until she acts" (Tremmel, 1993, p. 438). Schön, like Dewey (1929/1960), cautions against the "quest for certainty."

Ideally, reflection and social responsibility go hand in hand. Strike (1993) notes that virtuous and caring individuals have the potential to make the best educators, but that "character is a product of years, not credit hours" (p. 107). Therefore, he argues that in teacher education we cannot build character, but we may be able to develop "some degree of dialogical competence in the public moral language" (p. 107). By this he means that we may be able to help individuals think critically, analyze, reflect, and articulate their reasoning in acceptable civic (public) discourse—language that Strike terms "public moral language." Cases with a focus on specific contexts help individuals critically focus on their experiences and values and consider the consequences of actions and decisions with a view toward acting responsibly and professionally.

Tensions, Problems, and Conflicts

This book uses the vehicle of cases to stimulate analysis, encourage reflection, and spark discussion of numerous neglected aspects of teaching. The cases presented serve as the catalyst for reflection by presenting dilemmas in academic settings that contain tensions, problems, or conflicts and that call for action and/or resolution. Distinctions among tensions, problems, and conflicts are blurred, often cultural, and always personal. Determining when a problem becomes or will become a conflict is difficult. This book draws on the literature of conflict and often uses the word *conflict* as shorthand for a continuum that ranges from minor tensions to outright hostilities.

Conflict is part of life and is a complex, socially constructed concept. Each of us defines a situation as a conflict or not based on our experiences, personalities, cultures, and various other factors. Conflicts occur on many levels, ranging from interpersonal and personal to national and international. Conflicts in school settings may be among students, students and faculty, faculty and faculty, faculty and supervisors, individuals and institutions, and so on. Lebaron and Pillay (2006) define conflict as

> a difference within a person or between two or more people that touches them in a significant way. We all constantly encounter differences within and between ourselves and others. Only those differences that we perceive

as challenges to something we believe in or need, or to some aspect of our individual or shared identities, become conflicts. (p. 12)

Another definition of conflict by Perlow (2003) stresses that "conflict is not by nature good or bad. Conflict simply means difference—difference of opinion or interests" (p. 4).

In ESOL settings, and in the cases in this book, tensions, problems, and conflicts are often influenced by culture. Thandis (2009) notes that "cultural differences often cause miscommunications and conflict" (p. 18). Similarly, Mike (2009) argues that "ignorance of cultural diversity, not cultural diversity itself, is a source of disharmony and conflict in the global village" (p. 36). Indeed, the cross-cultural nature of teaching ESOL sets it apart from other instructional situations, providing numerous opportunities for miscommunication and misunderstanding and the dilemmas that go with them.

People are socialized to understand conflict in different ways. Lebaron and Pillay (2006) argue that culture and conflict are inextricable and that conflict occurs at three levels:

- the material level or the "what" of the conflict
- the symbolic level, the meaning of issues to the people involved, especially those meanings that resonate with peoples' identities, values, and worldviews
- and the relational level, or the dance among the parties, or the way in which conflict plays out (p. 19)

They argue that to resolve conflicts all three levels must be addressed and cultural understanding increased. Cultural understanding, Pillay (2006) contends, "begins with each of us committing to a process of increasing self-awareness, curious observation, ongoing reflection, and dialogue with others" (p. 55).

In this book, readers are asked to commit to a process of reflection, observation, and discussion: to become more aware of their own and others' perspectives. To promote cultural understanding, readers are asked to learn about other countries, cultures, and educational systems. Of course, each country has many cultures, there is wide variation among individuals within any given culture and country, and there is a danger of essentializing cultures, countries, and peoples. The importance of faculty members understanding each student and co-worker as an individual and each context as unique is stressed in this book. For example, a student may fail to turn in homework or a faculty colleague may be irritable or outright hostile for reasons unrelated to school or work. While trying to understand each individual and his or her perspective, learning about different cultures and countries can help place individual students and their perspectives within a broader cultural context. For example, knowing that certain educational systems foster different signs of respect for faculty or different student learning styles (e.g., Flaitz, 2003, 2006; Powell & Andersen, 1994; Reid, 1995) can help us understand students and their perspectives more fully while at the same time examining one's own perspectives. Increased cultural understanding can help prevent or resolve negative conflicts or turn them into constructive ones. Throughout his writings, Edward T. Hall called for promoting understanding of our own cultures and of the cultures of others. While we may never fully understand other cultures, Hall (1966) believes that being aware of the diversity of cultures can help us better understand our own culture and our own perspectives.

Tensions and conflict—whether they be interpersonal, intercultural, or cross-cultural—are daily occurrences. Ting-Toomey (1994) points out that intercultural conflicts often begin as miscommunication and that strategies for dealing with conflict may be influenced by culture and may vary from individual to individual. For example, what Perlow (2003) calls "silencing conflict" may be more common in some cultures and for specific individuals. In Asian cultures, students typically do not question the instructor or argue directly with classmates, whereas in other cultures questioning and arguing may be valued. In a work situation, a new employee may not tell a co-worker about the flaws he sees in a proposal for fear of disapproval or because he thinks that he cannot effect a change in the proposal. Perlow points out that once individuals silence themselves or are silenced, they are more reluctant to voice their views in the future. Perlow identifies this as the "silent spiral," which from Perlow's perspective—a Western one—is unhealthy for the individual. As a result, he or she may build up resentment of co-workers and lose interest in the project or job. This situation may ultimately be unhealthy for the organization.

Numerous books and articles, many for a popular audience, offer guidelines and methods for dealing with difficult people and situations and for handling conflict (e.g., Dana, 2001; Fisher & Ury, 1991; Scott, 2004). We offer a few general suggestions on page xvii for dealing with difficult situations whether they be minor annoyances, tensions, problems, or more extreme conflicts. These suggestions also constitute an approach we hope to foster in this book—a way of viewing situations and dilemmas using awareness, reflection, and dialogue. An overarching principle is to strive to be professional and humane in all our interactions with others.

1. Recognize that conflict (i.e., tensions and problems) is inevitable and simply a part of life.

2. Recognize that conflict can be constructive and is not always negative.

3. Recognize that individuals have different strategies for dealing with conflict, with some of these strategies influenced by culture, personality, and upbringing.

4. Cultivate self-awareness (e.g., of your feelings, perspectives, language, and behaviors).

5. Recognize that communication choices (i.e., verbal and non-verbal) are important. For example, in some cultures, refusing a request with a No threatens the face of others.

6. Cultivate awareness and understanding of others by listening without judgment and by creating an environment for open communication. Understand and respect the perspectives of others.

7. Help others save face.

8. Try to avoid taking others' comments and actions personally.

9. Recognize that with conflicts, people generally have strong feelings (such as anger, depression, and despair), and that, as Weisinger (1995) notes, it is often hard for an individual to hide emotions.

10. Recognize that the emotional state of an individual can be "caught" by others (what Weisinger, 1995, terms *emotional contagion* [p. 53]). "Emotional contagion" is especially important in group settings, so one must work to reduce and dissipate negative emotions. Often, this can be done simply by truly listening to others.

11. Recognize that an individual does not operate in a vacuum, but within a broader social context.

This last point highlights the interconnectedness of individuals, organizations, and societies. Ayers (2004) emphasizes the importance of the larger context and our interconnectedness when he writes that

> a just society creates the conditions for more of us to act more often in a moral way. . . . Everything good is not the simple result of individual virtue—there is also the matter of community ethics, of social ethics, the question of how we behave collectively, what our society assumes as normative and good. (p. 26)

Nonetheless, within the broader community, the individual is crucial to dealing with conflicts and in effecting change. Indeed, as educators, we believe that one person—an instructor—can make a difference, and we operate on that assumption each day. Educators, spiritual leaders, and activists all tell us we can change the world one person at a time (e.g., Clarke, 2003, 2007; Dalai Lama, 1999; Dalai Lama & Cutler, 2003; Freire, 1972). Each individual's actions matter.

Why Cases Are Useful

We were drawn to the issues presented in the cases in this book because of our experiences in the classroom; because of our interactions with colleagues, students, and supervisors; and because these issues are underrepresented in the TESOL literature. As we began to share our stories with others, colleagues and friends quickly related to our experiences and responded by telling us stories about dilemmas and conflicts in their own ESOL classrooms and academic institutions. Discussions of broad issues relating to conflict and culture in these contexts developed. We found stories to be powerful and an avenue into serious, frequently overlooked issues. Stories are compelling and help us make sense of our lives and work (e.g., Bruner, 1991). For all these reasons, cases are the core of this book, and we use them as a concrete way to deal with important educational issues.

Our belief in the value of using cases and stories is not unique. In fact, case methodology has a long history in law, medicine, business, and education. Christensen's two books (1981, 1987), presenting arguments for and guidance on using case methodology and actual cases for use, are perhaps best known, but there are those specific to education and TESOL (e.g., Egbert & Petrie, 2005). In addition to serving as instructional tools, case studies and personal narratives are used as qualitative research in fields such as anthropology, composition studies, and applied linguistics (e.g., Braine, 1999; Casanave & Schecter, 1997; Casanave & Vandrick, 2003; Yin, 2003, 2004).

No one case methodology exists; rather the pedagogical use of case studies takes many forms and can serve many purposes even within a single discipline. Similarly, the terminology also varies within and across fields. For the purpose of this book, we use the terms *case* and *case study* interchangeably to refer to a third person narrative of an event or sequence of events that is contextualized in time and place. In each case, human agency and intention are central. Our cases are based on true situations, but we have changed some details such as names and places. The cases are set in a variety of post-secondary ESOL settings in the United States, though many share similarities with other teaching situations. Each case, like situations that instructors encounter, is context-specific (i.e., local), complex, and multilayered. There is sometimes no right or easy answer to the dilemma presented.

Just as the definition of *case study* varies, so do the purposes for employing cases in teacher education and professional development. Cases have commonly been employed to teach (1) principles and theory, (2) precedents as practice, (3) morals or ethics, (4) strategies, dispositions, and habits of the mind, and (5) visions or images of the possible (Shulman, 1992, pp. 2–9). Whereas Shulman's classification of cases helps us explore their possible uses, the categories are not mutually exclusive; in fact, cases often can be used for multiple purposes.

The uses and advantages of using cases for professional development often overlap. In this book, cases serve as vehicles to address issues and situations that are underrepresented in the literature yet commonly encountered. Cases and stories are engaging and can be used to examine specific situations, important educational issues, and multiple perspectives. Cases present multiple levels of abstraction, promote the connection of theory with practice, lend themselves to the examination of literature in the field, and encourage personal and community reflection. Whereas teaching is a fundamentally cognitive act, a multitude of things go on in a classroom, many of which involve neither book knowledge nor intellectual approaches solely. Carter (1992) describes cases as "pedagogical puzzles." Kleinfeld (1992) argues that it is important to prepare teachers emotionally as well as intellectually for the kinds of situations they encounter in the classroom. Drawing on Dewey (1910), Zeichner and Liston (1996) emphasize that reflective action requires more than logic, problem-solving, and routine action when they say:

> When we reflect about students in our classrooms, we need to listen to and accept many sources of understanding. We need to utilize both our heads and our hearts, our reasoning capacities and our emotional insights. . . . In reflective action, in contrast to routine action, reason and emotion are engaged. (pp. 10–11)

Cases can provide such preparation for reflective action. Cases can never substitute for class observations, student teaching, practicum, or other professional experiences, but they provide identifiable experiences and snapshots of an instructor's work life.

Through critical thought and focused discussion of cases, individuals can create a discourse community where they can see, hear, and better understand others' perspectives, explore their own beliefs, analyze various approaches to a situation, and consider the consequences of various actions. Cases can help individuals be more open and mindful, can help them develop reasoning skills, and can help them begin to "think like a teacher."

With a focus on teaching professional ethics, Strike (1993) argues that examining case studies can develop skills in ethical reasoning, characterized as the ability to articulate moral reasoning in what he terms *public moral language*. He argues that gaining and improving such linguistic skills (what he terms *dialogical competence*) requires public forums dominated by ethical, not strategic, concerns. He also notes that although individuals may not initially articulate moral principles in examining a case, "they do recognize the importance of such considerations once they are pointed out" (p. 103) and can learn to analyze and articulate these considerations.

How to Use This Book

The primary perspective through which most of the cases in this book are presented is that of the classroom instructor yet, most cases also call for a wider perspective, involving views from students, administrators, institutions, and communities. Classroom instructors cannot operate in isolation but are connected to larger contexts. As Clarke (2007) says in describing an ecological perspective to teaching:

> In order to work effectively, the teacher-as-ecologist recognizes that the problems encountered on one level—the classroom, for example—are inextricably intertwined with elements of school policy and community politics. The ecologically minded activist realizes that problems are rarely solved at the level they are encountered. (p. 24)

Therefore, readers are encouraged to think about the broader perspectives in each case, and we have included some cases that explicitly involve an administrative perspective.

The cases are independent and can be read in any order; however, they are loosely ordered, beginning with classroom concerns and then progressing into concerns that move beyond the classroom into the larger world of students, colleagues, institutions, communities, and society. The cases typically introduce multiple issues, and the same or related issues may appear in several cases.

Cases present situations at the post-secondary level, including Intensive English Programs (IEPs), university-level instruction for matriculated students, community college programs, proprietary programs, and adult education classes. At first it may seem that these situations differ dramatically. In an IEP, students are generally full-time, either preparing to enter a degree program in a U.S. institution or studying English for professional or personal reasons. Students in these programs are generally in the United States on F-2 student visas and are well educated in their native languages. In addition, they may be more privileged (i.e., from upper middle- or upper-class families). This student profile also fits many of the matriculated students in undergraduate and graduate programs at U.S. universities who take English courses while they begin their degree programs. These are all full-time students whose main focus and obligation is studying. On the other hand, students enrolled in community colleges and adult courses tend to be immigrants or refugees who generally hold down one or two jobs and have family obligations. Unlike international students, they may have few opportunities to practice English outside of class and seldom have the same amount of time and energy to devote to learning English.

Despite these general differences, there are obvious connections among the situations that offer insight into the complexity of the teaching task. All of the students in these programs are adults who want to improve their English to better their circumstances, whether that entails getting a better job, understanding a child's English-speaking doctor, or getting a post-doctoral fellowship. In addition, all students are coping with a new environment, even those who have been in the country for several years. They bring very different cultural behaviors and expectations to the classroom. Moreover, many of us teach and work in these various environments at different points in our careers and often at the same time, for example, teaching classes at an IEP during the day and then teaching night classes at the local adult school.

These cases are based on our experiences and on stories we have heard from colleagues in post-secondary and adult mixed-language teaching situations in the United States. (Names, places, and other identifying details have been changed.) Even though the cases are drawn from educational environments in the United States, this book could also be used in post-secondary and adult English situations in other English-speaking countries such as the United Kingdom, Ireland, Australia, Canada, and New Zealand, as well as in classrooms in non–English speaking countries.

The primary audience for this book is individuals in teacher education classes, especially the practicum class or a methodology course. It can also benefit novice and experienced ESL faculty, volunteers, and instructional aides and be used in pre-service and in-service workshops for these groups. Although individuals can work through the cases independently, the best use of the book is as a springboard for discussion, thus allowing participants to benefit and learn from each other's research, experience, and thinking. The cases lend themselves to either small- or large-group face-to-face discussion or online discussion.

Each case is described and features several related extensions. A Matrix of Cases, delineating each case, title, and related issues follows this introduction. The featured case is followed by Questions for Discussion that ask the reader to examine the case from each stakeholder's perspective, focusing on the specific context in which the situation occurs. The next section, Extending the Case, presents several shorter cases that address similar issues with slight variations. Questions for Further Reflection raise broader questions about the general topic of the case. These are intended to stimulate both reflection and discussion that place the cases in broader social and cultural contexts. Delving Deeper contains suggested activities that require readers to go beyond the text, gathering information and resources in order to explore issues in greater depth. A list of resources is included following each case section. These resources may be helpful in working with the suggested activities in the Delving Deeper section. Finally, the actual resolution to the featured case is given followed by a prompt for reader reflection on that resolution.

The Nature of Cases

In working with the cases, readers are asked to keep several premises in mind. First, there is seldom one solution to a case. Multiple possibilities often exist, all seemingly valid and arguably good. At other times, there is no good resolution to a given case, with each possible action having many negative and few positive outcomes. This becomes evident when the resolution to the featured case is given. Some were resolved in what would be a positive manner. Other resolutions seem to present questionable choices, given available options, and a few cases actually seem to pose the poorest resolution possible. Perhaps, for this reason, numerous cases remain enigmatic. Sometimes there was no satisfactory resolution to the dilemma, and the problem continued or was ignored.

Readers are encouraged to think critically about each case and to reflect on the situation and case and evaluate the resolution. Differences of opinion related to the resolution are possible.

Part of the reality of teaching is that there are situations where the best course of action is not clear. This is true for any type of teaching but is especially relevant for situations where students come from a variety of different cultures. Few of us are well-versed in the cultural and educational mores of each student in our classes or are able to know each student's experiences, personality, and unique situations. Occasionally, after we have dealt with a dilemma, we must acknowledge that we did not handle it well. If we have made an obvious error, we need to remedy it as quickly as we can. In that case, it can be helpful to discuss the incident with colleagues to learn from the experience and to gain insights that can benefit us as well as other instructors. If time allows for reflection and discussion with others before dealing with a dilemma, we may be able to resolve the situation to benefit everyone.

Second, there are few hard-and-fast rules that dictate what one should do in all situations. Handling educational dilemmas cannot be learned by applying a checklist or following a set of prescribed rules. Gathering more information and reflecting carefully on a situation is often the best way to approach a classroom problem or crisis, but sometimes decisions need to be made on the spot. For example, a situation in which a student walks into class drunk is quite different from one in which an instructor feels that a particular female student is not participating in class because her culture does not encourage women to speak out. The first example requires immediate action while the other allows and calls for fact-finding, discussion with others, and longer reflection. Some situations seem to have only one or two possible immediate resolutions, while others may present several possible paths of action.

Finally, the cases included in this book are uneven in nature. Some reflect a relatively minor incident that could likely be resolved with appropriate dialogue and small adjustments in behavior. Others are microcosms of much larger issues in the field. For example, in Case 11 (Classroom Visitors), and its extension about an instructor who frequently brings a dog to class, there are obvious human relations problems and issues to be resolved, but they can probably be worked out amicably. In contrast, Case 37 (Linguistic Competence) raises several serious issues within the profession, such as the question of who can claim to be a native speaker, the advantages and disadvantages of having a native speaker as an instructor, and the increasing reality of English as a world language. The unevenness of the cases simply reflects the realities of teaching.

Suggestions for Instructors and Facilitators

The cases in this book are designed to foster discussion. Discussions can occur face-to-face in large classroom situations, in small groups, in pairs, or online. With large groups, there is an advantage in dividing into small groups because several different cases can be studied simultaneously, with each small group then reporting back to the larger group. This allows for everyone to be exposed to and think about more cases. Online discussions can occur in either a synchronous or asynchronous mode. Such online work can also serve as preparation for later face-to-face discussions, thus creating a blended learning environment. In all of these modes, participants need to agree to certain ground rules. First, everyone is an equal participant whose ideas are to be carefully listened to and respected. Second, participants reserve judgment and are open to new ideas and points of view. Third, participants use the opportunity to reflect on their own personal value systems and how they shape their reactions to the case. Fourth, participants need to articulate their reasoning by using respectful and civil discourse, what Strike (1993) terms *ethical reasoning,* characterized as the ability to articulate moral reasoning. Ideally individuals bring both heart and mind to the discussion. Edge (2002) asserts that "we learn by speaking, by working to put our own thoughts together so that someone else can understand them" (p. 19). In speaking as in writing, the act of articulating our thoughts and reasoning helps us to clarify them and gain insights into our values. The process of examining, reflecting on, writing about, and discussing and thereby learning from the cases, is the goal. Less important is arriving at complete agreement about what action or resolution is appropriate. Indeed, participants may never agree on the best way to deal with a given situation.

Before outlining possible approaches to using the cases either online or in class, we provide a few suggestions for instructors and facilitators.

1. View the learning environment as a laboratory where you and your students gain knowledge and insight.

2. Build an open, safe environment where individuals trust each other and are respected.

3. Be open to uncertainty in yourself and in your students. Allow yourself and others space to explore ideas.

4. Be prepared with ideas, additional questions, and more, but be willing to drop your plans to follow uncharted routes and free-flowing discussion.

5. Listen to each other with your heart and mind.

6. Focus on learning from your students and encouraging them to learn from one another. Keep in mind Alfred North Whitehead's comment, "What is really essential in your development you must do for yourselves" (cited in Christensen, 1987, p. 5).

It is important to emphasize participant preparation because it is far too easy to merely say or write, "This is what I think," with little or no reflection on the issues at hand. Here we outline possible approaches to using these cases, beginning with pre-discussion work. We give consideration to the different types of readers using this book and their instructional contexts. Through use and experimentation, you may modify or find other approaches that meet the needs of your specific audiences. We list numerous possibilities and do not envision all of them being used for any particular case. Indeed, you may wish to only focus on the featured case or the accompanying other components. We encourage you to be creative and adventuresome in utilizing the book's cases and accompanying apparatus. These suggestions apply to a group setting such as a class or workshop, an online community, or a blended community with online and face-to-face components.

Pre-Discussion Work

1. Give participants time to think, study, and ponder a featured case.

2. In a group setting or online, participants can be given time to read the case and look over the questions, make notes, or write out longer answers to the questions. For example, participants could be assigned a featured case and come to class ready for discussion. If it is a workshop setting, participants can be given time to do this on the spot or beforehand.

Possibilities for Discussion of a Featured Case

1. In a group setting, ask participants to role-play the situation.

2. In a group setting or online, ask individuals to take on the persona of specific characters and explain their feelings, views, and actions from their persona's perspective.

3. In a group setting or online, divide individuals into small groups and assign each group a few of the discussion questions. Each group can then post or orally explain their responses to the larger group.

4. In online settings, individuals can be asked to respond to one or more postings by their colleagues so that there is a discussion.

5. Advise students not to look at the resolution to the featured case until all the work has been completed.

Possibilities for Extending the Case

1. Participants need time to read, study, and ponder the cases before discussing them. Participants should consider how the extended cases relate to the featured case.

2. Online or in group settings, groups or individuals can be assigned specific cases to present to the larger community (online or face-to-face). Others can then discuss the case.

3. Participants can be asked to respond to one or more cases in a written reflection. This reflection can be shared with others or simply submitted to the facilitator.

4. The cases can be role-played or individuals can take on the persona of different characters and explain their feelings and views.

Possibilities for Questions for Further Reflection

1. Facilitators, instructors, or individual readers can pick and choose which questions to focus on. The goal here is to place the issues in a broader context and increase understanding of the complexity of the issues.

2. Some of the same activities listed can be used. Individuals need to articulate their views and their reasoning online, in writing, or in face-to-face discussions. The interaction with others is important. These questions provide the opportunity to focus previous discussions and activities and place them in a larger context.

Possibilities for Using Delving Deeper

1. Keep in mind that these activities are designed to broaden readers' knowledge of the situations and help them revisit their earlier thoughts and reflections.

2. Initial work on these activities in most cases will need to be done outside the classroom or in group settings because they require research.

3. Online or in group settings, divide the activities among the participants, assigning specific groups to report back to the larger group.

4. Written group or individual reports may be assigned. With written work, the facilitator needs to give specific guidelines as to general format, length, and documentation form. For example, for an M.A. TESOL practicum class, the instructor may require that responses be double-spaced, be three to four pages, and be in APA format with a reference list. For less-structured situations, participants may be asked to simply give the author, title, and date of a specific reference.

5. In short workshops or informal situations, the facilitator may wish to bring in the necessary material or modify the activities to suit a given situation.

Resolution to the Case

To initiate readers' thoughts on the resolution, a small space after the resolution is provided where users can make notes about the implications of what did happen and/or list what they would have done. This makes the book a handy reference once teachers are practicing.

An additional activity to consider is having participants write their own cases based on their own experiences or based on interviews with practicing teachers. We suggest that individuals work through several of the cases before attempting to write their own. We also advise instructors and facilitators to provide guidelines for developing cases, including (1) basing the case on something that has actually happened; (2) avoiding real names; (3) not revealing a resolution; and (4) avoiding personal prejudices in the case.

Finally, while these suggestions assume that there is an instructor or a facilitator and groups of individuals who use this book together, this book and these suggestions can benefit individuals. We encourage individual readers to form a discussion group that meets in person or online to informally discuss the cases in a less structured setting such as in the office, while commuting to work, or over lunch. We also encourage readers to connect the cases to their own experiences and knowledge, to consider writing their own stories, and to share their ideas with others.

This book explores the gray areas and dilemmas of teaching ESOL in post-secondary and adult contexts, largely in the United States. Although ethical issues are only one aspect of this book, Daniel Terris's (2005) argument is apropros: "By its nature, ethics resists completion and closure. Rules and codes and cases tend to reduce ethics to a checklist, rather than a process of self-examination that explores grey areas and intractable dilemmas" (p. 153). Exploring these gray areas and situations through cases will not necessarily bring closure to the issues, tensions, and conflicts that they raise, nor will it teach readers how to handle all dilemmas, tensions, and conflicts encountered in ESOL contexts. Grappling with these cases will, however, actively involve readers in the process of reflection and honest discussion, teach us about ourselves, broaden perspectives, and enhance our ability to handle dilemmas with thought, professionalism, and social responsibility.

REFERENCES

American Educational Research Association (AERA). (1992). *Ethical Standards of the American Educational Association.* www.aera.net

Ayers, W. (2004). *Teaching toward freedom: Moral commitment and ethical action in the classroom.* Boston: Beacon Press.

Braine, G. (Ed.). (1999). *Non-native educators in English language teaching.* Mahwah, NJ: Lawrence Erlbaum.

Bruner, J. (1991). The narrative construction of reality. *Critical Inquiry, 18,* 1–21.

Carter, K. (1992). Toward a cognitive conception of classroom management: A case of teacher comprehension. In J. H. Shulman (Ed.), *Case methods in teacher education* (pp. 111–130). New York: Teachers College Press.

Casanave, C. P., & Schecter, S.R. (Eds.). (1997). *On becoming a language educator: Personal essays on professional development.* Mahwah, NJ: Lawrence Erlbaum.

Casanave, C.P., & Vandrick, S. (Eds.). (2003). *Writing for scholarly publication: Behind the scenes in language education.* Mahwah, NJ: Lawrence Erlbaum.

Christensen, C. R. (1981). *Teaching by the case method.* Boston: Harvard Business School.

———. (with Hansen, A. J.). (1987). *Teaching and the case method: Text, cases, and readings.* Boston: Harvard Business School.

Clarke, M. A. (2003). *A place to stand: Essays for educators in troubled times.* Ann Arbor: University of Michigan Press.

————. (2007). *Common ground, contested territory: Examining the roles of English language teachers in troubled times.* Ann Arbor: University of Michigan Press.

Cohen, R. (2003). *The good, the bad & the difference: How to tell right from wrong in everyday situations.* New York: Broadway Books.

Dalai Lama. (1999). *Ethics for the new millennium.* New York: Riverhead.

Dalai Lama, & Cutler, H.C. (2003). *The art of happiness at work.* New York: Riverhead.

Dana, D. (2001). *Conflict resolution: Mediation tools for everyday worklife.* New York: McGraw-Hill.

Dewey, J. (1910). *How we think.* Boston: D.C. Heath.

————. (1960). *The quest for certainty: A study of the relation of knowledge and action.* New York: Capricorn Books. (Original work published 1929)

Edge, J. (2002). *Continuing cooperative development: A discourse framework for individuals as colleagues.* Ann Arbor: University of Michigan Press.

Egbert, J., & Petrie, G. M. (2005). *Bridge to the classroom: ESL cases for teacher exploration* (Volume 3: Adult contexts). Alexandria, VA: TESOL.

Fisher, R., & Ury, W. (with Patton, B. [Ed.]). (1991). *Getting to yes: Negotiating agreement without giving in* (2nd ed.). New York: Penguin.

Flaitz, J. (Ed.) (2003). *Understanding your international students: An educational, cultural, and linguistic guide.* Ann Arbor: University of Michigan Press.

————. (2006). *Understanding your refugee and immigrant students: An educational, cultural, and linguistic guide.* Ann Arbor: University of Michigan Press.

Freire, P. (1972). *Pedagogy of the oppressed* (M. B. Ramos, Trans.). London: Penguin.

Hafernik, J. J., Messerschmitt, D. S., & Vandrick, S. (2002). *Ethical issues for ESL faculty: Social justice in practice.* Mahwah, NJ: Lawrence Erlbaum.

Hall, E. T. (1966). *The hidden dimension.* Garden City, NY: Doubleday.

Johnston, B. (2003). *Values in English language teaching.* Mahwah, NJ: Lawrence Erlbaum.

Kleinfeld, J. (1992). Learning to think like a teacher: The study of cases. In J. H. Shulman (Ed.), *Case methods in teacher education* (pp. 33–49). New York: Teachers College Press.

Lebaron, M., & Pillay, V. (Eds.). (2006). Conflict, culture, and images of change. In *Conflict across cultures: A unique experience of bridging differences* (pp. 11–23). Boston: Intercultural Press.

Mike, Y. (2009). "Harmony without uniformity": An Asiacentric worldview and its communicative implications. In L. A. Samovar, R. E. Porter, & E. R. McDaniel (Eds.), *Intercultural communication: A reader* (12th ed.), (pp. 36–48). Boston: Wadsworth Cengage Learning.

NAFSA: Association of International Educators. (1989). *NAFSA's Code of ethics.* www.nafsa.org

National Educators Association (NEA) (1975). *Code of Ethics of the Education Profession.* www.nea.org/aboutnea/code.html

Perlow, L. A. (2003). *When you say yes but mean no: How silencing conflict wrecks relationships and companies . . . and what you can do about it.* New York: Crown Business.

Pillay, V. (2006). Culture: Exploring the river. In M. Lebaron & V. Pillay (Eds.), *Conflict across cultures: A unique experience of bridging differences* (pp. 25–55). Boston: Intercultural Press.

Powell, R. G., & Andersen, J. F. (1994). Culture and classroom communication. In L. A. Samovar & R. E. Porter (Eds.), *Intercultural communication: A reader* (7th ed.), pp. 322–331. Belmont, CA: Wadsworth Publishing.

Reid, J. M. (Ed.) (1995). *Learning styles in the ESL/EFL classroom.* New York: Heinle & Heinle.

Schön, D. A. (1983). *The reflective practitioner: How professionals think in action.* New York: Basic Books.

Scott, G. G. (2004). *A survival guide for working with humans: Dealing with whiners, back-stabbers, know-it-alls, and other difficult people.* New York: Amacon.

Shulman, L. S. (1992). Toward a pedagogy of cases In J. H. Shulman (Ed.), *Case methods in teacher education* (pp. 1–30). New York: Teachers College Press.

Strike, K. A. (1993). Teaching ethical reasoning using cases. In K. A. Strike & P. L. Ternasky (Eds.). *Ethics for professionals in education: Perspectives for preparation and practice* (pp. 102–116). New York: Teachers College Press.

Terris, D. (2005). *Ethics at work: Creating virtue at an American corporation.* Waltham, MA: Brandeis University Press.

Thandis, H. C. (2009). Culture and conflict. In L. A. Samovar, R. E. Porter, & E. R. McDaniel (Eds.), *Intercultural communication: A reader* (12th ed.), (pp. 18–28). Boston: Wadsworth Cengage Learning.

Ting-Toomey, S. (1994). Managing intercultural conflicts effectively. In L. A. Samovar & R. E. Porter (Eds.), *Intercultural communication: A reader* (7th ed.), (pp. 360–372). Belmont, CA: Wadsworth.

Tremmel, R. (1993). Zen and the art of reflective practice. *Harvard Educational Review, 63*(4), 434–458.

Weisinger, H. (1995). *Anger at work.* New York: Willam Morrow.

Yin, R. K. (2003). *Case study research: Design and methods* (2nd ed.). Thousand Oaks, CA: Sage.

———. (2004). *The case study anthology.* Thousand Oaks, CA: Sage.

Zeichner, K. M., & Liston, D. P. (1996). *Reflective teaching: An introduction.* In D. P. Liston & K. M. Zeichner (Series Eds.), *Reflective teaching and the social conditions of schooling: A series for prospective and practicing teachers.* Mahwah, NJ: Lawrence Erlbaum.

MATRIX OF CASES

Case	Title	Issues
1	Adjusting to a New Environment	culture shock; navigating new systems and environments; homesickness; excitement with new situation; discrimination
2	Group and Pair Work	setting up group and pair work; evaluating group and pair work; interpersonal relationships; gender
3	Interpersonal Interactions among Students	interactions among individual students; politeness; student complaints and negative comments about others; prejudice; providing and receiving peer comments and criticism
4	Students and Political Issues	political differences; debating respectfully; peaceful classroom and safe environment; taboos; non-verbal communication and politeness; prejudice
5	Student Classroom Behaviors	appropriate classroom behavior; politeness and respect for others; classroom management, rules, and discipline; feelings of entitlement
6	Class Participation	nonverbal communication; paying attention in class; affective filter and monitor; student personalities
7	Intracultural Behavior	individualistic and collectivistic cultures; peer pressure; saving face
8	Reasonable and Unreasonable Excuses	academic procrastination; cultural values and practices; determining what is and is not an acceptable excuse; verifying excuses; Gay, Lesbian, Bisexual & Transgender (GLBT) issues; feelings of entitlement; cancelling class
9	Attendance and Punctuality	student honesty; cultural concepts of time; excused vs. unexcused absences
10	Student Misunderstandings	determining if misunderstandings are linguistic or cultural; speech acts and cultural differences; student accusations of faculty error
11	Class Visitors	power differential between students and instructor; procedures and etiquette for visiting classes; program policies regarding visitors; pets

12	Third Party Involvement	cultural variations in use of third parties; understanding appropriate use of third parties in new environment
13	Student Attire, Hygiene, and Mannerisms	cultural attitudes toward personal mannerism, attire, and behavior; determining appropriate attire, mannerisms, and behaviors for specific settings; faculty bringing up sensitive issues with individuals and/or classes; faculty responding to insensitive or personal comments students make about a classmate or classmates
14	Student Disabilities and Mental Health	incorporating students with disabilities and mental health issues into the class; making appropriate accommodations for individuals with disabilities; identifying individuals who may need assistance because of a disability or mental health issue
15	Risky Behaviors	identifying students who may engage in risky behaviors; determining when and how to intervene; determining faculty responsibility for students to adopt healthy habits and avoid risky behaviors; drawing attention to individual students' behaviors
16	Stress	academic stress; personal stress; assisting students with stress; overachievers
17	Religious Beliefs and Practices	discussing controversial issues; expressing strongly held beliefs; promoting religious understanding and tolerance among students; creating a safe environment for all students and faculty; verifying legitimacy of requests
18	Discrimination	discrimination against and by students and faculty; stereotyping based on culture, gender, sexual identity, and other characteristics; confidentiality of student information and specific incidents; determining how best to assist students who have been discriminated against
19	Technology and Modern Life	uses of technology to enhance language learning; accessibility of technology by students; students' and faculty's comfort in using technology; privacy issues
20	Cheating	differing cultural understandings of cheating; consequences of cheating; honor code
21	Plagiarism	understanding what plagiarism is; different cultural views of need to document scholarship

22	Assigning Course Grades	consideration of personal issues when calculating course grades, or approving grade changes or withdrawals; gift-giving; criteria and weight of each component in calculating course grades
23	High-Stakes Testing	admission criteria of colleges and universities and their appropriateness; gatekeeping mechanisms; stress associated with high stakes testing
24	Parental Pressure and Influence	faculty consideration of parental expectations and pressure when making decisions; autonomy of faculty; faculty determining appropriate advice and assistance for students under pressure
25	Requests for Academic Assistance	faculty burnout; faculty setting limits and maintaining good "work-life balance"; institutional support services for students
26	Recommendations	deciding whether to write a letter of recommendation or act as a reference; determining what to tell a student about the content of the letter; determining what to include in a letter; confidentiality of student information; legal considerations regarding information included in letters of recommendation
27	Sponsored Events	politeness; types of sponsored events; service-learning; role of instructor before, during, and after sponsored events; racism
28	Students and the Legal System	U.S. Immigration and Customs Enforcement (ICE); institutional responsibilities related to federal regulations; verifying student explanations; helping students understand U.S. government regulations
29	Dangerous and Uncomfortable Situations	crimes; incorporating safety issues into the curriculum; community resources for safety; respecting others' personal decisions
30	Possible Abusive Situations	identifying abusive situations: determining how to deal with suspected abusive situations; community resources for dealing with abuse
31	Selecting Materials	criteria for the appropriateness of materials; respecting different faculty and pedagogical perspectives; determining how the choices of materials impact other classes and students

32	Faculty Personal Agendas	academic freedom; content-based instruction: sharing of personal information and political views in classes; advocacy
33	Faculty Personal Issues	dealing with complaints about an instructor; interpreting Americans with Disabilities Act (ADA); impact of family obligations and other personal issues on work; handling faculty with suspected substance abuse problems
34	Romance at School and Work	power differential among faculty, staff, and students; dating among faculty or staff and students; handling unwanted attention from classmates and/or instructors; verifying rumors; privacy
35	Collegiality	working well with others; being considerate and reasonable; taking one's responsibilities seriously; power differential among faculty
36	Integrity	student evaluations of teaching; honesty and ethical behavior of faculty in presenting themselves and in dealing with others
37	Linguistic Competence	qualifications of faculty; students' perceptions of faculty qualifications and effectiveness; non-native speaker (NNS) of English professionals and native speaker of English (NSE) professionals; accents; discrimination
38	Instructor Effectiveness	qualifications of an instructor; professional responsibilities and obligations; methods of grading written work; pacing of instruction; dealing with mixed-level classes
39	Students as Research Subjects	protection of research subjects; quality and appropriateness of research; research etiquette
40	Job Security and Support at Work	working conditions; job security; professional development; issues particular to part-time instructors

Case 1 · Adjusting to a New Environment

Several weeks into the semester, one morning during break, An Trang speaks to her writing instructor, Ms. Ito. She explains that Bao Nguyen, her Vietnamese classmate, is unable to come to class today and has asked her to hand in his writing homework. Ms. Ito asks if Bao is ill and An hesitates but then says, "Yes, he is very homesick, but his parents insist that he stay, learn English, and then go to graduate school in the U.S." She continues by describing his situation in more detail. He rents a room off campus but spends most of his time alone. Because of this situation, he is unable to attend class or concentrate on his studies. He can't sleep at night and has trouble eating American food. An explains that she is very worried about him because, even though he has gone to the doctor and is taking medication to help him sleep, he is unable to sleep more than a few hours every night. Ms. Ito remembers that he has missed many classes, and when he is there he seems distracted and has difficulty focusing. In fact, he often seems to have trouble keeping his eyes open. Ms. Ito thanks An for submitting Bao's paper and for explaining Bao's situation. She asks her to please tell Bao that the teachers are concerned about him and would like to help him.

Questions for Discussion

1. What additional information would help you better understand this case?

2. How do you think An feels about Bao and his situation before she talk to Ms. Ito?

3. How do you think Ms. Ito feels about Bao and his situation?

4. How can Ms. Ito or anyone discover what the "real" issues affecting Bao are? For example, is Bao simply suffering from culture shock?

5. What options does Ms. Ito have in dealing with Bao's situation? Evaluate each option.

1

Extending the Case

Consider the four situations presented. Then reflect on these questions: (1) How does each situation differ from or relate to this case? (2) What contributing factors come into play in each situation? and (3) What are the possible courses of action for each?

1. Each week in her U.S. Culture class, an instructor allows 10 minutes for general student questions regarding U.S. culture. One week two unrelated questions arise. First, several students ask why some U.S. college women wear short shorts, short skirts, and blouses that don't cover their midriffs to class whereas others seem to wear pajamas and slippers to class. They ask why professors allow students to attend class dressed this way. Other students make the comment that Asian toilets are more sanitary than Western toilets and that this seems particularly true of public restrooms. The students go on to describe in detail the cleanliness or lack of cleanliness in the bathrooms in the residence halls.

2. Before class one day, a student from the People's Republic of China is talking to her classmates about tipping in the United States. They all agree that it is very confusing to know when and how much to tip because in many countries people do not leave tips. She asks about tipping taxi drivers. When the instructor enters the class, they ask her about tipping taxi drivers. The instructor explains that it is customary in the U.S. to tip taxi drivers about 15 to 20 percent. The student is puzzled and explains that she took a taxi and it cost $12.00. She gave the driver a $20 bill, and he didn't give her change.

3. One evening during break, an instructor hears several Somali women talking about their children's school and teachers. They value education and feel it is the way for their children to succeed in the United States. However, they are unable to help their children with their studies and do not understand the U.S. educational system. For example, they ask each other, "What is this parent-teacher conference?"

4. Before the beginning of class on Monday, the instructor joins a conversation with a group of students who are talking about their weekend activities. One student from Argentina explains that she went out with friends to several bars on Friday night, shopped and took

a sightseeing tour on Saturday, and attended the Gay Pride parade and festivities on Sunday. She continues to list activities that she has planned for the following days and weeks. She exclaims that she loves her roommate, loves everything about the United States, and loves all the friendly people, especially the handsome men.

Questions for Further Reflection

1. List four or five aspects of a new environment that may be different from one's usual environment (e.g., food, transportation system).

2. Which of these aspects may be difficult to adjust to? Why? Which ones may be easy to adjust to? Why?

3. Drawing on your initial list, which aspects seem most appropriate to discuss in class? Why?

4. How can faculty recognize when students are not adjusting well? How can faculty assess the seriousness of the difficulties?

5. List four or five ways that faculty can assist students who are having adjustment problems.

6. What are three or four ways that faculty can assist students in achieving a balance between their social lives (e.g., making new friends, exploring the sights of the areas, having new experiences) and their academic studies?

7. List two or three activities that allow faculty to introduce and discuss differences among cultures in terms of daily activities (e.g., tipping, transportation system, bureaucratic procedures) without making value judgments.

Delving Deeper

1. *Culture shock* is a term often applied to initial adjustment to a new environment. To what extent does it seem an appropriate term? How is culture shock generally defined, and what are the usual stages of adjustment? Have you ever experienced culture shock? Using the Internet and other resources, find definitions and examples. Write about your findings and your experiences. If you like, include a figure showing the stages of culture shock, either one you create or one you find. Document your sources appropriately. Be prepared to share your findings as well.

2. Think of times that you have been in other countries, cities, or even cultural areas where you were unsure of the customs or how things were done. Think of friends or relatives that you know who have traveled abroad or experienced adjusting to a new environment or culture. How did you and others adjust? What factors seem important to successful adjustments? Make a list of factors, and explain each. Use the Internet and other resources to check and revise your list. Share your list with others either in writing or in discussion. Document your sources.

Resources

DeCapua, A., & Wintergerst, A. C. (2004). Culture shock. In *Crossing cultures in the language classroom* (pp. 105–144). Ann Arbor: University of Michigan Press.

Hess, J. D. (1997). *Studying abroad/learning abroad: An abridged version of the whole world guide to culture learning.* Boston: Intercultural Press.

Ogami, N. (Producer). (1987). *Cold Water* [DVD]. Boston: Intercultural Press.

Stori, C. (2001). *The art of crossing cultures* (2nd ed.). Boston: Nicholas Brealey.

Thomas, K., & Harrell, T. (1994). Counseling student sojourners: Revisiting the U-curve of adjustment. In G. Althen (Ed.), *Learning across cultures* (pp. 89–107). Alexandria, VA: NAFSA.

Torbiörn, I. (1994). Dynamics of cross-cultural adaptation. In G. Althen (Ed.), *Learning across cultures* (pp. 31–55). Alexandria, VA: NAFSA.

Worldwide Classroom: Consortium for International Education & Multicultural Studies. www.worldwideedu/travel_planner/culture_shock.html.

Resolution to the Featured Case

After class, Ms. Ito sent Bao an email, expressing her concern for his well-being and encouraging him to speak to her privately. She also spoke to Mr. Youngblood, the director of the IEP, about Bao's situation. Mr. Youngblood asked that Ms. Ito ask Bao to come and speak to him when he returned to class. Mr. Youngblood also checked with each of Bao's instructors about his performance. Bao generally missed the morning classes, telling his instructors that he couldn't sleep at night and then couldn't get up for class. He generally was attending the afternoon classes. All the teachers said he seemed tired and distracted. When Bao met with Mr. Youngblood later that week, he was obviously distraught and tired from lack of sleep. Based on their conversation and information from faculty, Mr. Youngblood made an appointment for Bao with a counselor on campus. After several counseling sessions, Bao and the counselor convinced his parents that he needed to return to Vietnam for health reasons. With the help of Ms. Ito, Mr. Youngblood, and the counselor, Bao officially withdrew, left the program, and returned home within a month of An's speaking to Ms. Ito about Bao's situation.

MY THOUGHTS on the Resolution

Case 2 Group and Pair Work

Mr. Jack Thompson teaches a high-level, oral communication skills class at a midsize private university. He is a firm believer in the benefits of group work because it provides students with more opportunities to practice their English and prepares them for the realities of the workplace, where working well with others as a team is crucial. He often assigns students to groups by having them count off one by one for the total number of groups needed. In addition to short, in-class group projects, he assigns a semester-long, culminating group project. Each member of the group receives the same grade. In their groups, students are expected to select and investigate one aspect of life in the United States, have the topic approved by the instructor, and then prepare a final 20-minute oral group presentation for the class, as well as a 10–15 page written report. All group meetings after the initial one are held outside of class.

About halfway through the semester, Wolfgang Hauer from Germany makes an appointment to see Mr. Thompson. Wolfgang says that after beginning their research on the topic of eldercare in the United States, three of the other group members have asked him to serve as a spokesperson. They request that one member of the group, Alberto Giovanni from Italy, be removed from the group and assigned to a different group. Their complaint is that Alberto simply does not fit in with the other members. When assigned a task from the group, he brings back sloppy, inaccurate work. In addition, he is unfriendly in group interactions. They all feel that he is a misfit. Mr. Thompson has also observed that Alberto is a loner and not very popular with the other students. Mr. Thompson tells Wolfgang that he appreciates his willingness to come and speak with him, but that he will need a day or so to think about the situation.

The next day, much to Mr. Thompson's surprise, Alberto arrives during office hours. He asks to be removed from his group because the members of his group are unfriendly to him, and they do not value his hard work. He adds that he does not like group work at all and asks to work on an independent project so that the teacher can better evaluate his ability.

Questions for Discussion

1. What additional information would help you better understand this case?

2. How do you think Wolfgang and the other members of the group feel, beyond the stated reasons, about working with Alberto? Why?

3. What other reasons could Alberto have for wanting to leave the group?

4. Is Mr. Thompson's method of assigning group members a good one? Why or why not?

5. How might other groups react if Mr. Thompson changes the composition of the groups once the work has already started?

6. What options does Mr. Thompson have for assigning a grade to Alberto?

7. What are the advantages and disadvantages of each of these options?

Extending the Case

Consider the two situations presented. Then reflect on these questions: (1) How does each situation differ from or relate to this case? (2) What contributing factors come into play in each situation? and (3) What are the possible courses of action for each?

1. In a pronunciation class, the instructor frequently makes group assignments and requires group presentations. One of his favorite topics is American National Parks. One group with students from Spain, Italy, and Indonesia gives a report on Zion National Park, accompanied by a visual and musical computer presentation. The Indonesian student, the weakest speaker in the group, does not speak at all, since he agreed that it would be in everyone's best interest for him to work on the technical aspects of the presentation. After class, the instructor talks to the group and finds out that the Indonesian student did all of the computer work for the audio and visual part of the presentation. The group members, including the Indonesian student, explain that his English is not as fluent as theirs and they decided that this was a fair allocation of the work. The presentation was excellent.

2. An instructor of Business English frequently uses pair work in his English for Special Purposes (ESP) class. He feels that pair work simulates the workplace environment with its give-and-take interaction typical of corporate America. At the beginning of the semester, he pairs off the students by selecting one student from the back of the room and one from the front. At the end of the first class, a student from Dubai asks to speak privately with the instructor. He requests that he be assigned only male partners.

Questions for Further Reflection

1. What are the advantages and disadvantages of group work? Of pair work?

2. What types of projects and assignments lend themselves best to group work? To pair work? Explain your answers.

3. Give three examples of activities that work well with groups. Give three examples of activities that work well with pairs.

4. What factors should instructors consider when deciding whether to (a) assign students to groups and pairs, (b) allow students to form their own groups and pairs, or (c) use a system of random selection?

5. What are the advantages and disadvantages of each of the above modalities?

6. What are some options for dealing with students with special requests regarding group and pair work?

7. If an instructor decides to assign students to pairs (as opposed to allowing students to do it themselves), what are some pedagogical reasons for pairing these individuals?

   a. a shy yet grammatically accurate student with a more talkative student who is often inaccurate

   b. students who are best friends

   c. students from different language groups

   d. students from the same language group

   e. the highest-performing student with the lowest

   f. students with approximately the same overall proficiency

   g. two female students

8. What are some strategies to help ensure equitable participation in group activities? In pair work?

9. What are some strategies for evaluating and grading group work and pair work?

10. What role might familiarity with group and pair work, or lack of it, play in students' reactions to such work in U.S. classrooms?

11. How can instructors explain the importance of pair and group work to students?

Delving Deeper

1. Group and pair work are common in U.S. educational institutions. Students from other countries may or may not be familiar with these educational modalities. Even if they have done group or pair work, they may or may not be as comfortable with the style and types of activities assigned in the U.S. Consult the Internet or the two Flaitz resources cited regarding teaching practices in other countries. Select two or three countries to research. Write about your findings. Be prepared to discuss them with others.

2. Evaluating and assessing pair and group work is often difficult. Consult the Internet on this topic using descriptors such as "ESL group work," and "ESL collaborative learning." Look for suggestions on how to evaluate students. Feel free to use other descriptors in the search box. Then select one of these options: (a) Find two different suggestions for assessing students. Describe these options and discuss the advantages and disadvantages of each. Cite your sources. (b) Speculate about why there is a paucity of information on evaluating students engaged in group work and pair work. Write about some strategies that you might use for evaluating students.

Resources

Brown, H. D. (2001). Interactive language teaching II: Sustaining interaction through group work. In *Teaching by principles: An interactive approach to language pedagogy* (2nd ed.), (pp. 176–191). White Plains, NY: Pearson.

Flaitz, J. (Ed.). (2003). *Understanding your international students: An educational, cultural, and linguistic guide*. Ann Arbor: University of Michigan Press.

———. (2006). *Understanding your refugee and immigrant students: An educational, cultural, and linguistic guide.* Ann Arbor: University of Michigan Press.

Long, M. H., & Porter, P. (1985). Group work, interlanguage talk, and second language acquisition. *TESOL Quarterly, 9,* 207–228.

Nisbett, R. E. (2009). Living together versus going it alone. In L. A. Samovar, R .E. Porter, & E. R. McDaniels (Eds.) *Intercultural communication: A reader* (12th ed.), (pp. 134–145). Boston: Wadsworth Cengage Learning.

Oxford, R. (1997). Cooperative learning, collaborative learning, and interaction: Three communicative strands in the language classroom. *The Modern Language Journal, 81,* 443–456. Special Issue: Interaction, collaboration and cooperation: Learning languages and preparing language teachers.

Resolution to the Featured Case

Mr. Thompson noticed that Alberto could not get along with any of the other students. They seemed to avoid him and often rolled their eyes when he spoke in class because his responses were long and wordy, often off the subject. Taking these observations into consideration, Mr. Thompson determined that it was best for everyone to allow Alberto to work independently for the rest of the semester.

MY THOUGHTS on the Resolution

Case 3 Interpersonal Interactions among Students

In her low-intermediate writing class in an IEP, Ms. Nichols often pairs students to provide peer feedback on their essays. Before doing it for the first time, she briefly talks about the need to be respectful of others and their work. She prepares peer response sheets with up to 5 questions for students to answer, always including "What did you like best about this paper?" One semester, she has a mixed class, with Europeans, Asians, Middle Easterners, and Hispanics. She feels that students like each other and generally work well with each other. One day she pairs Cindy Kim from Seoul with Pierre LaRoche from Paris. While reading each other's papers, Cindy repeatedly comments to Pierre that she has trouble reading his handwriting, and then she laughs. A short while later, Pierre begins muttering, "Stupid. This is stupid. I cannot believe this is so stupid. You are a stupid girl." Visibly upset, Cindy begins to cry and leaves the class. Ms. Nichols is on the other side of the room, helping another pair of students, when the incident happens. However, she hears what Pierre says and sees how shaken Cindy is. There are only a few minutes remaining until the end of class, so Ms. Nichols asks students to hand in their essays and peer response sheets and dismisses them. She asks Pierre to stay after class and speak with her.

Questions for Discussion

1. What additional information would help you better understand this case?

2. How might Pierre feel about Cindy's comments about his handwriting? How might Cindy feel about Pierre's comments?

3. What factors might have contributed to the misunderstanding between Pierre and Cindy (e.g., differences in gender? maturity? culture? linguistic ability? other factors?)?

4. What, if anything, could Ms. Nichols have done to avoid this situation?

5. What type of preparation for the class as a whole seems advisable when having students peer edit, critique each other's work, or share their work with classmates?

6. How can positive feedback be useful in peer editing?

7. What steps can Ms. Nichols take to minimize the likelihood of such situations occurring in her classes in the future? Between Pierre and Cindy? Among other students?

8. Who else, if anyone, could benefit from knowing about this incident (e.g., other faculty? the IEP director?)?

9. What options does Ms. Nichols have for dealing with this situation? Evaluate each option.

Extending the Case

Consider the three situations presented. Then reflect on these questions: (1) How does each situation differ from or relate to this case? (2) What contributing factors come into play in each situation? and (3) What are the possible courses of action for each?

1. Students in a community college class frequently laugh good-naturedly at one of the lowest-performing students in the class, a male student from Japan. The Japanese male takes on the role of class clown.

2. An outgoing Chilean woman complains to the instructor in her IEP that the other students in the class are unfriendly and not nice to her. She accuses them of ignoring her and never picking her as a partner. She seems upset and begins crying when explaining her feelings to the instructor.

3. In an adult evening class, a male student from the Middle East refuses to work with a specific female student from Asia, saying that her English is poor and that she is impossible to understand.

Questions for Further Reflection

1. List situations in which peer feedback can be useful. Briefly explain each of these situations. For example, does peer feedback seem appropriate for oral as well as written work?

2. How can instructors help students provide useful comments and constructive criticism to others? List some possible approaches and explain each one. Do these approaches differ for written and oral work?

3. Think of two or three class activities that instructors can use to help students become better able to handle and respond to peer comments, jokes, and criticisms.

4. What are some ways for instructors to help students be respectful of each individual in the class? Explain and evaluate each.

5. Suggest two or three ways that instructors can address educational, cultural, and gender differences in giving and receiving criticism.

6. How can instructors handle students who are intentionally or unintentionally disrespectful of a classmate in class?

7. What options does an instructor have for dealing with a situation in which two students in the class obviously dislike each other? Where one student dislikes one or more other students?

Delving Deeper

1. Typical classrooms and typical classroom activities often differ from country to country and culture to culture. Therefore, students in an ESL class often have varying degrees of familiarity with commenting on others' written or oral work. Writing textbooks and texts on speaking often offer advice for instructors on how to structure peer editing activities and peer evaluation of speeches. Textbooks often include peer evaluation sheets for written work and/or for speeches. Look at two or three ESL or English textbooks to see what advice and specific guidance they give for peer evaluation and editing. Compare one writing textbook to one on speaking. What features do the peer evaluations for written work and for oral presentations share?

2. Research politeness strategies in English by finding lessons and exercises in ESL textbooks and/or online. You may wish to focus on politeness in requests, compliments, greetings, or other specific speech acts or functions. Choose one or two lessons and evaluate them. What suggestions would you make to improve the lessons? Write your evaluations and be prepared to share them with others.

Resources

Benesch, S. (1984). *Improving peer response: Collaboration between teachers and students.* (ERIC Document Reproduction Service No. ED243113)

Brown, P., & Levinson, S. C. (1987). *Politeness: Some universals in language usage (Studies in Interactional Sociolinguistics 4).* New York: Cambridge University Press.

Dave's ESL Café. www.eslcafe.com.

Hafernik, J. J. (1983). *The how and why of peer editing in the ESL writing class.* (ERIC Document Reproduction Service No. ED 253064)

———. (1995, June). Promoting cultural sensitivity among students. *Global Issues in Language Education Newsletter, 19.* http://jalt.org/global/publications.htm.

Internet TESL Journal. http://iteslj.org.

Lakoff, R. (1973). The logic of politeness, or minding your P's and Q's. In C. Corum, T. C. Smith-Stark, & A. Wiser (Eds.), *Papers from the Ninth Regional Meeting of the Chicago Linguistic Society* (pp. 345–356). Chicago: Chicago Linguistic Society.

———. (1990). Politeness. In *Talking power: The politics of language* (pp. 34–39). New York: Basic Books.

Rollinson, P. (2005, January). Using peer feedback in the ESL writing class. *ELT Journal, 59*(1), pp. 23–30.

Resolution to the Featured Case

Ms. Nichols spoke to Pierre about being respectful and courteous at all times, especially when peer editing. Pierre was defensive, arguing that Cindy had said his handwriting was bad and that her ideas were indeed "stupid." Ms. Nichols was frustrated and asked the IEP director to speak to Pierre. The director asked other faculty who had Pierre and Cindy in their classes about their interactions and learned that they seemed fine even after their disagreement. The faculty members said that it seemed obvious that they were not friends outside of class, however they were not hostile to each other in class. The director asked Pierre to speak to her. Once again Pierre was defensive. The director explained to Pierre that the word **stupid** in English is considered rude when describing people and ideas. She emphasized that she did not believe that Pierre had intended to be impolite. She also defined the term **constructive criticism** and advised Pierre to consider how his comments might be interpreted. Pierre listened without making comments.

MY THOUGHTS **on the Resolution**

Case 4

Students and Political Issues

In a pre-MBA program for international students at a major university, Ms. Browne teaches an oral communication module. Ms. Browne, an experienced instructor, works closely with the MBA faculty to identify the skills most important to success in the program and in the international business world. One essential skill is debating: supporting one's opinion and refuting others' counterarguments.

Thus, Ms. Browne frequently assigns debates to her class. The current topic is the pros and cons of beauty pageants. The Miss America Pageant recently took place, and there were several articles in the local newspaper about it. To introduce the idea, Ms. Browne holds a general class discussion before having the students prepare for the formal debate. In this case, she begins by asking the students if they know anything about the pageant. Wan Shenjun, a recent arrival from China, confidently raises his hand and states that the authorities in China banned such pageants because they are demeaning to women. He completely agrees with his government's stance on the issue. Soani, a vocal student from Tonga, interrupts by stating, "Your government is wrong. There is no problem with beauty shows. We often have them. There is no problem. We even have them for men."

Questions for Discussion

1. What additional information would help you better understand this case?

2. To what extent did Ms. Browne set up the debate activity well?

3. How might an instructor prepare students for a debate so that they are less likely to take counterarguments from peers personally?

4. Some students in this case have clearly indicated a point of view before the debate. What are some reasons for assigning them to the side they feel strongly about? What are some reasons for assigning them to debate the other side?

5. How might Ms. Browne handle an opinionated political comment such as Soani's ("Your government is wrong")?

Extending the Case

Consider the three situations presented. Then reflect on these questions: (1) How does each situation differ from or relate to this case? (2) What contributing factors come into play in each situation? and (3) What are the possible courses of action for each?

1. A graduate student from Estonia gives an oral presentation about how his country was nearly shut down electronically for two weeks after an extended spam sabotage incident. He states that it was certainly the Russians who masterminded this devious plot, and the remainder of his talk consists of a list of reasons why the Russians who currently live in Estonia should be forced to relocate.

2. At a local community college, the instructor asks students to identify issues they would like to discuss during the semester. One student suggests they discuss U.S. immigration policies. In explaining why he suggested this topic, the student says it is wrong for immigrants to wave Mexican flags when demonstrating to change U.S. immigration policies. He adds that most of those people are probably illegal, can't speak English, and should be deported immediately. Several other students disagree with his statements and the noise level in the classroom increases.

3. In giving informational presentations on their countries in a speaking class, one student from the People's Republic of China concludes his speech by saying that someday Taiwan will be reunited with the PRC as Taiwan rightfully belongs to China. The Taiwanese students in the class are surprised by this comment.

Questions for Further Reflection

1. How can an instructor encourage students whose countries are or were in conflict to cooperate in a class?

2. What are the arguments for or against placing students from the same country of origin in different sections of a course, when multiple sections are offered?

3. What are the differences between an argument and a discussion? What are some ways to keep the discussion of a controversial topic from becoming an argument?

4. List some ways an instructor can deal with student work (e.g., papers, oral reports, journal entries) when the work, which starts with solid factual information, eventually drifts into a diatribe, based totally on personal opinion.

5. How can instructors help students understand the types and uses of evidence in scholarly work? List several examples.

6. In what ways can instructors help students truly listen to their classmates and others with whom they may disagree?

7. What are two or three things an instructor can do to build a safe, caring, and respectful classroom environment?

Delving Deeper

Discussing controversial issues, and even the choice of issues to discuss, is personal and often cultural. This means that people may come to a discussion or debate with very different ideas about what subjects are open for discussion and what behaviors and language are or are not appropriate. Keep this in mind as you approach the following activities:

1. Make a list of subjects for discussion that may be controversial or even taboo. Resist the temptation to declare that nothing is taboo anymore. (For example, it would be difficult to ask your dentist how much money he or she earned last year.) Then either interview two or three individuals from other countries to find out what they would put on their lists of taboo topics, or consult the Internet or the works by Flaitz cited in the list of Resources to find information on other countries and cultures. Add this information to your list and compare the subjects. What types of issues are on the lists?

2. Given that controversial and taboo subjects often must be discussed, think of several ways to avoid personal attacks and confrontation. You may want to consider the following: (a) volume and tone of voice, (b) humor, (c) word choices, (d) terms of address, (e) body language, (f) types of evidence used, (g) acknowledgment of counterarguments and refutation, and (h) turn-taking. Using the Internet or the list of Resources at the end of this chapter, research the types of strategies used in other cultures to discuss controversial subjects. Write a comparison and be prepared to discuss your findings.

3. Examine several ESL listening and speaking textbooks. Determine which ones cover discussion skills (e.g., agreeing and disagreeing). What activities do these textbooks include so that students can practice these skills? Prepare a chart and be ready to discuss your findings.

Resources

Flaitz, J. (Ed.). (2003). *Understanding your international students: An educational, cultural, and linguistic guide.* Ann Arbor: University of Michigan Press.

———. (2006). *Understanding your refugee and immigrant students: An educational, cultural, and linguistic guide.* Ann Arbor: University of Michigan Press.

Johnstone, B. (1989). Linguistic strategies and cultural styles for persuasive discourse. In S. Ting-Toomey & F. Korzenny (Eds.), *Language, communication, and culture* (pp. 139–156). Newbury Park, CA: Sage.

Maurice, K. (1986). Cultural styles of thinking and speaking in the classroom. In P. Byrd (Ed.), *Teaching across cultures in the university ESL program* (pp. 39–50). Washington, DC: NAFSA.

Moskowitz, G. (1978). *Caring and sharing in the foreign language class: A sourcebook on humanistic techniques.* Cambridge, MA: Newbury House.

Noddings, N. (1984). *Caring: A feminine approach to ethics and moral education.* Berkeley: University of California Press.

Tannen, D. (1999). The roots of debate in education and the hope of dialogue. In *The argument culture: Stopping America's war of words* (pp. 256–290). New York: Ballantine.

TESOLers for Social Responsibility Caucus. www2.tesol.org/communities/tsr.

Resolution to the Featured Case

Ms. Browne stopped her class and began to discuss some basic guidelines for debating, emphasizing that debates must be grounded in fact, not opinion. She then pointedly asked both students to evaluate their own comments as to whether they were closer to fact or opinion. Eventually both men realized that their statements were based largely on personal opinion.

MY THOUGHTS **on the Resolution**

Case 5

Student Classroom Behaviors

Mark Chandra teaches a high-intermediate reading and writing course at a language school in a large city. He has a good rapport with his students, is easy going, and is well-respected. One semester he has a particularly difficult class in that students often arrive late, tend to chat in class, and often do not submit work on time. Throughout the session, Abdullah Khan and Manzoor Gul have been especially troublesome in that they socialize with their neighbors in class, fail to pay attention to the lesson, and ignore Mr. Chandra's repeated requests to stop talking and pay attention. Additionally, they sometimes speak Arabic loudly across the classroom or in the hallway during the class break. Over the course of the session, Mr. Chandra has spoken to them numerous times privately about their classroom behavior, their absences, and their poor performance in class, as they often fail to turn in work or turn it in late. Mr. Chandra has also spoken to the class on several occasions about the need to arrive on time, turn in work on time, and be attentive in class.

After Abdullah and Manzoor are absent for several days, they return to class, with Abdullah arriving late. During the two-hour class, Mr. Chandra repeatedly asks them to stop talking and to focus on their work. They stop for a short while and then begin chatting again. Finally, Mr. Chandra has had enough and tells Manzoor to leave the class as he is being disruptive. Mr. Chandra escorts Manzoor out of the class and briefly explains that he has been rude and disruptive and cannot stay in the class that day. Mr. Chandra then returns to class and completes the lesson. After class, Abdullah speaks to Mr. Chandra saying, "I don't like you anymore. I used to like you, but not anymore. How could you kick Manzoor out of class? You better not do that to me." Mr. Chandra is upset from the whole experience and unclear about Abdullah's meaning. Shortly after class, Manzoor comes to see Mr. Chandra in the teacher's room and apologizes for his behavior in class.

Questions for Discussion

1. What additional information would help you better understand this case?

2. How do you think Mr. Chandra feels during and after this particular incident?

3. How do you think Manzoor feels, having been told to leave class?

4. How do you think Abdullah feels about the incident? How do you interpret his statements to Mr. Chandra after class?

5. How do you think Mr. Chandra interprets Abdullah's comments?

6. How do you think the other students in the class interpret the incident involving Abdullah and Manzoor, and Mr. Chandra's actions (i.e., asking Manzoor to leave the class)?

7. What are the advantages and the disadvantages of Mr. Chandra's actions?

8. What options does Mr. Chandra have for responding to Manzoor's apology? Evaluate each option.

9. When Manzoor returns to class, how should Mr. Chandra treat him and evaluate his future work? If his behavior is appropriate? If it is still problematic?

10. What can Mr. Chandra do to minimize the likelihood of such disruptive incidents happening again in this class? From happening in future classes?

Extending the Case

Consider the four situations presented. Then reflect on these questions: (1) How does each situation differ from or relate to this case? (2) What contributing factors come into play in each situation? (3) What are the possible courses of action for each?

1. In a community college course, the instructor notes in the syllabus that students should turn off their cell phones and all electronic devices. Despite this instruction, students' cell phones sometimes ring during class. When a cell phone goes off, the instructor asks the student to

turn it off and the student does, often apologizing. One day, a Thai woman's cell phone rings, and she answers it in class, saying to the class, "Today is my birthday, so I'm going to take this call." She then walks out of class speaking Thai on the phone.

2. During student presentations in a speaking class, the instructor notices that one student is sending text messages and not listening to his classmate's speech. Another student is reading the newspaper.

3. During a three-hour class, from 9:30–12:30 AM, the instructor always gives students a 15-minute break. The instructor allows students to bring drinks and light snacks to class. However, two students always come back late from break with full meals (e.g., bowls of cereal, pancakes, or hot entrées) and proceed to enjoy them during the last part of the class.

4. A young instructor, Agnes Schneider, confides to a colleague that two of her students address her inappropriately; a Japanese student simply uses her last name, saying, "Hello, Schneider," and a Chinese student calles her by her first name, saying, "Hello, Agnes." She has repeatedly told the class to call her Ms. Schneider or Professor Schneider. Most students follow her request.

Questions for Further Reflection

1. How can instructors introduce appropriate classroom behavior to students?

2. List reasons a student may act inappropriately in class.

3. What consequences seem appropriate for adult classroom misbehavior (as opposed to child classroom misbehavior)?

4. When reprimanding students, how can faculty be sensitive to students' need to save face and avoid embarrassment?

5. At what point does it seem appropriate for an instructor to seek support from an administrator in dealing with a disruptive student?

6. What does it mean to maintain discipline in a classroom? Can this term be defined differently depending upon the culture and situation?

7. Describe classroom situations in which, in your opinion, the instructor is too concerned with being in control and other situations in which the instructor is not concerned enough about discipline.

8. What are possible reasons a faculty member may be lax in maintaining discipline in a classroom (e.g., fear of poor student evaluations, indecision about what to do)?

9. How does an instructor's reluctance or failure to maintain discipline in a classroom affect other students in the class?

10. Describe a classroom situation that you would consider out of control. In such a situation, what options does an instructor have?

Delving Deeper

1. Assumptions about what is appropriate classroom behavior vary according to country, culture, and educational experience. Add one or two behaviors to each column in the chart—behaviors that are generally considered appropriate in U.S. academic settings and behaviors that are generally considered inappropriate in U.S. academic settings. Then think of classroom behaviors that are acceptable in the U.S. but not in another country. Be prepared to discuss your examples. How might this chart be different for other countries and cultures?

Appropriate Classroom Behaviors	Inappropriate Classroom Behaviors
Raising one's hand to ask a question or speak	Talking to classmates when the instructor is speaking
Addressing the instructor by last name unless told his or her first name can be used	Doing homework for another class
Maintaining eye contact with the instructor or student speaker	Standing when the teacher enters the classroom

2. Faculty often include class rules and policies on their course syllabi. Some may develop a contract, with or without student involvement, that outlines expected behaviors. A common term for such contracts is *behavior contracts*. Then faculty may require each student to sign the contract, with faculty keeping the original and giving each student his or her signed copy. Examine two or three course syllabi for specifics about expected behaviors, and examine a behavior contract. Then draft a behavior contract for a specific educational setting (e.g., IEP, community college, adult school). Indicate the educational setting and cite any sources you use.

3. Search websites such as Dave's ESL Café or another source for tips on such issues as classroom management, rules, and discipline. List four or five examples of misbehavior by adults and four or five suggested consequences. Do the consequences seem appropriate? Explain your answer. Present your findings in a chart and be prepared to discuss them. Cite your sources appropriately.

Resources

Archer, C. (1994). Managing a multicultural classroom. In G. Althen (Ed.), *Learning across cultures* (Rev. ed.), pp. 73–87. Washington, DC: NAFSA.

Brown, H.D. (2001). Classroom management. In *Teaching by principles: An interactive approach to language pedagogy* (2nd ed.), (pp. 192–206). White Plains, NY: Pearson.

Crookes, G. (2003). Classroom management in ES/FL teachers' practice. In *A practicum in TESOL: Professional development through teaching practice* (pp. 141–160). New York: Cambridge University Press.

Dave's ESL Café. www.eslcafe.com.

Levine, D. R. (1993). Education: Values and expectations. In *Beyond language: Intercultural communication for English as a second language* (pp. 205–238). New York: Prentice Hall.

Powell, R. G., & Andersen, J. (1994). Culture and classroom communication. In L. A. Samovar & R. E. Porter (Eds.), *Intercultural communication: A reader* (7th ed.), (pp. 322–330). Belmont, CA: Wadsworth.

Resolution to the Featured Case

Later that afternoon Mr. Chandra went to see the director of the program to tell her of the incident and to ask her advice. When he arrived, the director told him that two students had spoken to her about the incident; one was Manzoor and another was a Tibetan student not involved in the incident. She asked Mr. Chandra what had happened and if he was okay; she said the students seemed concerned about him because his actions seemed out of character. Mr. Chandra explained the situation, giving a broader, more detailed picture than the students had although basically the same as the students' account. He and the director talked about the specific incident but focused more on how to proceed with the class and how to deal with disruptive students in general and the particular ones in his class. When Mr. Chandra asked her directly, the director told him that he could ask a disruptive student to leave the class. She also offered to speak to any student if he wanted her to.

Abdullah and Manzoor were less disruptive in the following classes. After about a week, they stopped attending class altogether.

MY THOUGHTS **on the Resolution**

Case 6   Class Participation

Over the summer, Mr. Fullmark, an experienced IEP instructor, develops some new strategies for working with his high-level oral communications class. He wants to incorporate some of the exercises used in drama to help his students speak more slowly, enunciate more clearly, project their voices, and ultimately speak with more confidence. To this end, he develops several games and role-play activities. On the first day of class in the fall semester, he meets his group. The class is fairly small with four Japanese women, two Thai men, an African man, and a woman from Taiwan. After the introductions, Mr. Fullmark explains his goals for the semester and how he plans to incorporate a lot of activities that require verbal interaction. The class members all nod in agreement. He then asks for questions. There are none, so he decides to begin with the first activity to build some class momentum from the beginning. He divides the class into two teams and asks each group to stand in a corner of the classroom, diagonally across from each other. He hands each group a list of sentences, a blank piece of paper, and a pen. The first member of the team must read the first sentence to the other team across the room in a very loud voice so that the team can hear it well enough to write it down correctly. The activity is going well until it is Masako Kato's turn to read a sentence. She simply looks around at everyone and says, "No, no, no." She gives the script to the next member of her team.

Questions for Discussion

1. What additional information would help you better understand this case?

2. What are some possible explanations for Masako's behavior?

3. How do you think the other students view Masako's behavior?

4. How do you think Mr. Fullmark views Masako's actions?

5. In what ways do you think Masako's actions affect the overall group spirit of the class?

27

6. What are some ways for instructors to evaluate class participation?

7. How can Mr. Fullmark take individual personalities and cultural habits into consideration when evaluating class participation?

8. How can Mr. Fullmark structure class activities to allow for different types of participation?

9. What options does Mr. Fullmark have in this case to encourage Masako's participation?

Extending the Case

Consider the three situations presented. Then reflect on these questions: (1) How does each situation differ from or relate to this case? (2) What contributing factors come into play in each situation? and (3) What are the possible courses of action for each?

1. A husband and wife from Poland are in the same class. They always sit together. Whenever the instructor asks the wife a question, the husband quickly answers for his wife, seldom allowing her to formulate her own answers and comments.

2. A gregarious student from Greece always calls out an answer before the other students have a chance to raise their hands. His answers are often incorrect.

3. A Chinese student helps his friend whose English is weak by translating what the teacher says into Chinese and whispering it into his ear. The weaker student never volunteers to answer a question. He only answers when called on. In addition, he rarely makes eye contact with the instructor.

Questions for Further Reflection

1. To what extent should instructors require oral, in-class participation from students in a speaking class? In a writing class? In other types of classes?

2. What kinds of student behaviors, apart from speaking, could instructors consider as active participation in class?

3. What are the advantages and disadvantages of having active participation count as part of a student's course grade for both the students and the instructor?

4. What are some nonverbal indicators that a student is actively participating in class?

5. What role does eye contact play in defining active participation?

6. When is it acceptable for a student to be silent in class?

7. What are some cultural differences in educational systems that may influence participation in class? (For example, think about how you have answered questions about what constitutes participation in the U.S. What behaviors in class are expected? Are these same behaviors expected as signs of participation in other cultures?)

8. How might gender differences influence class participation? Socio-economic differences?

9. What steps can an instructor take to insure that all students have an equal opportunity to participate in class, including speaking?

10. List several techniques that can be used to encourage students to actively participate in class.

Delving Deeper

1. Observe an ESL class and, for about 15 minutes, make notes of the ways students indicate, nonverbally, that they are paying attention and actively participating in class even though they may be silent. Describe their behaviors either orally or in writing.

2. In the same class, or another one, spend about 15 minutes looking for indicators that a student or students are not paying attention and thus not participating (e.g., they are looking out the window, reading, etc.). Describe these behaviors and then suggest some ways the instructor might pull the distracted students back into active attention to the classroom activities.

3. Learn about Stephen Krashen's (1982) theories regarding second language acquisition. How do the terms *monitor* and *affective filter* help explain student behaviors in the featured case and the extensions? Develop definitions of these terms and then speculate about Masako's situation. In this instance, you may wish to look at the resolution to the case first.

Resources

Buzzelli, C. A., & Johnston, B. (2002). Participation, representation, and identification: Culture and morality in classrooms. In *The moral dimensions of teaching: Language, power and culture in classroom interaction* (pp. 80–117). New York: Routledge.

Cardozo, L. F. (1994). Getting a word in edgewise: Does "not talking" mean not learning? *TESOL Journal, 4*(1), 24–27.

Flaitz, J. (Ed.). (2003). *Understanding your international students: An educational, cultural, and linguistic guide.* Ann Arbor: University of Michigan Press.

———. (2006). *Understanding your refugee and immigrant students: An educational, cultural, and linguistic guide.* Ann Arbor: University of Michigan Press.

Hall, E. T. (1959). *The silent language.* New York: Doubleday.

Krashen, S. (1982). *Principles and practice in second language acquisition.* Oxford: Pergamon Press.

Morita, N. (2004). Negotiating participation and identity in second language academic communities. *TESOL Quarterly, 38,* 573–603.

Norton, B. (2000). *Identity and language learning: Gender, ethnicity and educational change.* New York: Pearson.

Reitzel, A. C. (1986). The fear of speaking: Communication anxiety in ESL students. In P. Byrd (Ed.), *Teaching across cultures in the university ESL program* (pp. 127–130). Washington, DC: NAFSA.

Tsui, A. (1996). Reticence and anxiety in second language learning. In K. M. Bailey & D. Nunan (Eds.), *Voices from the language classroom* (pp. 145–167). New York: Cambridge University Press.

Vandrick, S. (2000). *Language, culture, class, gender, and class participation.* Paper presented at the annual meeting of TESOL, Vancouver, British Columbia, Canada. (Eric Document Reproduction Service No. ED 473086)

Resolution to the Featured Case

Mr. Fullmark talked to Masako right after class. She was not really able to explain why she could not participate. They agreed that perhaps Masako was just overwhelmed by everything that was new. Mr. Fullmark told her that she had to participate in class, but for the first week or so, he would not call on her directly until she became more comfortable in class. After the first month, Mr. Fullmark called on her regularly. She answered questions briefly, directly, and in a very quiet voice. Mr. Fullmark felt that she improved over the course of the semester, but overall, he was not happy with her progress and wished he could have gotten her to express herself more freely.

MY THOUGHTS on the Resolution

Case Intracultural Behavior

Ms. Lawlor teaches intermediate and advanced ESL classes in an art academy in a large city. The academy is a private school and includes coursework and degree programs in fine arts, commercial art, illustration, graphics, and fashion design. Each year a number of international students are admitted to the academy. A large program has developed because the English language entrance requirements are fairly low compared to those of a college or university. The skills to be learned, namely, art, do not require as high a level of English proficiency as other more traditionally academic courses of study. Each year, Ms. Lawlor has several students from Korea in her class, and she repeatedly notices some interesting trends in their behavior. Often the Korean women are very quiet in class, always deferring to one dominant Korean man.

One particular semester it is Mr. Park. For example, he usually speaks on behalf of all Korean students, this time telling Ms. Lawlor that the reading assignment is too long. Whenever a Korean student is absent, Mr. Park always explains the reason. One day in reading Mr. Park's journal, Ms. Lawlor makes note of an entry he has made regarding the dress design of a fellow Korean student, Ms. Kim. It states, "I'm going to kill that fat pig. She copied my design."

Questions for Discussion

1. What additional information would help you better understand this case?

2. What are some possible explanations for Mr. Park's behavior?

3. What are some possible explanations for the Korean women's silence in class?

4. What cultural dynamics seem to be operating in this classroom?

5. How can Ms. Lawlor encourage each student to participate?

6. What options does Ms. Lawlor have in dealing with Mr. Park's journal entry? Evaluate each option.

7. What options does Ms. Lawlor have in dealing with Mr. Park's influence over the other Korean students? Evaluate each option.

Extending the Case

Consider the two situations presented. Then reflect on these questions: (1) How does each situation differ from or relate to this case? (2) What contributing factors come into play in each situation? and (3) What are the possible courses of action for each?

1. A Taiwanese woman is having academic difficulties and is advised by her instructor to study more. The instructor tries to give her some tips on when she might be able to study. The student mentions that over the weekend the other Taiwanese students on campus are planning an all-day picnic. The instructor advises studying instead, but the Taiwanese student says that she cannot do that because then the other Taiwanese will know that she is not very smart.

2. Two Israeli men, about the same age, constantly back each other up in class. If one says something, the other corroborates it. If one makes an error, the other comes up with a situation in which the utterance could be plausible.

Questions for Further Reflection

1. What should an instructor do when one student clearly dominates the classroom interaction? When two students from the same language background dominate the interaction?

2. To what extent are dominating behaviors in class and derogatory comments in a personal journal equally problematic? Should they be addressed in the same way?

3. List several examples of intracultural behavior in the classroom. Which might be problematic? Which ones do not seem problematic?

4. Referring to the list above, what are some ways to handle intracultural behaviors that are problematic?

5. How can an instructor help students speak for themselves and at the same time show the deference required by their own cultural norms?

6. How can an instructor help students resist the negative influence of peers from their home country?

Delving Deeper

1. What is a good working definition of *saving face*? Is this concept operative in most cultures? Does it play out differently in different cultures? What is a good working definition of *peer pressure*? How are saving face and peer pressure related? Try to think of a situation from your own educational experience in which peer pressure influenced your behavior or thinking. Did it work in a positive or detrimental way? Write a description of the scene and describe what happened. Might it be considered an example of saving face?

2. Researchers sometimes discuss cultures as falling along a continuum of individualistic to collectivistic. While we do not wish to essentialize cultures, these concepts can be useful in helping us understand behaviors and values. Using appropriate resources, define these terms. How can the distinction be helpful in understanding the patterns of behavior in the featured case?

Resources

DeCapua, A., & Wintergerst, A. C. (2004). More on culture. In *Crossing cultures in the language classroom* (pp. 50–104). Ann Arbor: University of Michigan Press.

Folb, E. A. (1994). Who's got room at the top? Issues of dominance and non-dominance in intracultural communication. In L. A. Samovar & R .E. Porter (Eds.), *Intercultural communication: A reader* (7th ed.), (pp.131–139). Belmont, CA: Wadsworth.

Goffman, E. (1967). *Interaction ritual*. Garden City, NY: Doubleday.

Kale, D. W. (1994). Peace as an ethic for intercultural education. In L. A. Samovar & R. E. Porter (Eds.), *Intercultural communication: A reader* (7th ed.), (pp. 435–440). Belmont, CA: Wadsworth.

Nelson, G. (2000). Individualism-collectivism and power distance: Applications for the English language classroom. *CATESOL Journal, 12*(1), 73–91.

Pashby, P. (2002). *Korean intracultural influences on interaction in adult ESL classes: A case study.* Unpublished doctoral dissertation, University of San Francisco.

Resolution to the Featured Case

Ms. Lawlor responded to Mr. Park in his journal about the inappropriateness of his entry, specifically calling another student "a fat pig." It did not happen again. In addition, she talked to him about his classroom behavior. He indicated that he understood, and his behavior changed for about a week.

MY THOUGHTS **on the Resolution**

Case 8 Reasonable and Unreasonable Excuses

Mr. Bolton stresses vocabulary acquisition in his intensive English reading and writing class for high-intermediate students. Over the years, he has become aware of how a limited vocabulary holds back even his brightest students. Therefore, he has students keep vocabulary notebooks that he collects regularly, spends class time on word derivations and formation, and gives frequent vocabulary quizzes on words from the class readings and discussions. He always announces the day of the quiz, gives the quiz during the first ten minutes of class, and tells students the correct answers immediately after collecting their papers.

One day two students arrive late, just as Mr. Bolton has finished going over the answers for the quiz. After class these two students, Mustafa Jawi and Eugenia Ognovienko come up to Mr. Bolton's desk and say, "We have time now and will take the vocabulary quiz we missed. Should we take it in the classroom or come to your office with you?" Mr. Bolton does not immediately reply.

Questions for Discussion

1. What additional information would help you better understand this case?

2. Do you think Mr. Bolton should ask why the two students were late to class? Do they owe him an explanation?

3. How do you think Mr. Bolton feels about the students' request to take the vocabulary quiz?

4. Why do you think the students feel entitled to take the vocabulary quiz even though they were late for class?

5. What are some possible reasons the students were late? Which excuses might be considered legitimate?

6. What could Mr. Bolton have done in previous classes to reduce the likelihood of such requests?

7. How do you think the other students would feel if they learned that the students who missed the quiz were permitted to take it later?

8. What options does Mr. Bolton have for dealing with this situation? Evaluate each option.

Extending the Case

Consider the three situations presented. Then reflect on these questions: (1) How does each situation differ from or relate to this case? (2) What contributing factors come into play in each situation? and (3) What are the possible courses of action for each?

1. In the last few weeks of the semester, a Brazilian student asks her instructor to let her turn in journal entries for several weeks that had been due four to six weeks before. The student says that she has been having personal problems because she recently came out as a lesbian to her friends and family. She adds that most of her friends have been supportive, but her family and two close friends are very upset and actually angry.

2. A student from Singapore emails and phones the instructor after the scheduled final exam, explaining that he was confused about the day and time of the final. He apologizes repeatedly and asks if he can take the final exam at another time.

3. The Thanksgiving holiday is next week and matriculated students at the university ask their writing instructor if she can cancel their class on Wednesday afternoon before Thanksgiving. The instructor explains that they must have class since the Thanksgiving holiday does not begin until Thursday. She notes that they have a four-day weekend, as Friday is also a holiday. She reminds students that they have the first draft of an essay due Wednesday and that she is obligated to hold all scheduled classes. The students continue to strongly argue their case, explaining that all their other university professors have cancelled classes. If other professors have, why can't she? The instructor does not want students to be angry and hostile and later give her poor evaluations or be uncooperative. She is confused about what to do.

Questions for Further Reflection

1. What are the advantages and disadvantages of an instructor's having firm deadlines for students' submitting homework, essays, and other work and for not allowing students to make up missed work?

2. In what, if any, situations do firm deadlines seem unnecessary or overly rigid? Explain your answer.

3. What effect does it have on a class and its students if the syllabus says *no late papers,* but the instructor makes exceptions and often allows students to turn in papers late?

4. If an instructor has a policy that work cannot be made up, what are some examples of legitimate exceptions? How can an instructor ensure that a policy and its exceptions are fairly and justly applied?

5. What are the advantages and disadvantages of allowing students to miss or drop one quiz or paper per semester with no questions asked? For faculty? For students?

6. What are the advantages and disadvantages of a program-wide policy, as opposed to individual classroom policies, regarding (a) make-up tests, and (b) late papers? For faculty? For students?

7. How can an instructor assess the truthfulness of an excuse? When is it appropriate for an instructor to request documentation regarding an excuse?

8. What are some legitimate reasons for an instructor to cancel class?

9. What option does an instructor have if few students attend class the day before a long holiday or near the end of the semester?

Delving Deeper

1. Conduct research using the Internet or print sources to find the definition of *academic procrastinator.* Think of your own experience as a student. Have you known any academic procrastinators? Write your definition of the term and give examples. If possible, use your own experiences. Be prepared to share your definition and examples with others.

2. Different cultures and countries often place value and importance on particular practices and behaviors. Due to cultural differences, what is considered a reasonable excuse in one country or culture may not seem reasonable in another. For example, in some cultures, family obligations are more important than one's obligations as a student. As a result, a student may think that skipping class or failing to submit homework because her parents are in town is a legitimate excuse, whereas in the United States many faculty would not consider that a legitimate excuse. Make a list of wide-ranging excuses for failing to complete assigned work or for missing deadlines. List excuses that you have used or heard about as well as ones you make up. Be creative. (If you have trouble making your list, search on the Internet using keywords such as *academic procrastinator.*) Then interview several people, preferably from different countries and/or cultures, and ask them to place each excuse in the appropriate column: (a) reasonable, (b) borderline, or (c) unreasonable. Analyze the responses and include your opinions. Write about your findings and be prepared to share them orally with others.

3. Find scenes from movies, episodes from TV shows, or videos on websites (e.g., YouTube) in which an individual provides an excuse for a particular action or behavior. Describe and analyze the examples. Write your analysis and share it with others.

Resources

Academic Tips. www.academictips.org.

Kadison, R., and DiGeronimo, T. F. (2004). *College of the overwhelmed: The campus mental health crisis and what to do about it.* San Francisco: Jossey-Bass.

Lowes, R., Peters, H., & Stephenson, M. (2004). *The international student's guide: Studying in English at university.* Thousand Oaks, CA: Sage.

Resolution to the Featured Case

Mr. Bolton was taken aback by Mustafa's and Eugenia's assumption that they could take the vocabulary quiz they had missed because they were late. He reminded them that vocabulary quizzes given in class could not be made up and that this fact was stated on the syllabus. He also reminded them that it had been announced in previous classes that there would be a vocabulary quiz at the beginning of class. They protested that they had had trouble finding a parking place. He urged them to come to class on time in the future, allowing ample time to find a parking place. He also encouraged them to keep track of scheduled quizzes. Finally, he noted that the lowest of their quiz grades would be dropped, so the zero on this quiz would not count.

MY THOUGHTS **on the Resolution**

Case 9   Attendance and Punctuality

Seiji Nakamura from Japan is absent from class on Monday and Tuesday. He returns on Wednesday and asks to be excused for both Monday and Tuesday. His instructor, Mrs. Mokes, asks why he was absent. Her attendance policy is that all absences must be accounted for. Unexcused absences result in a lowered grade. Seiji says he was sick, so Mrs. Mokes excuses the absences and asks that in the future he send an email to let her know when he cannot come to class. Later that day, she happens to overhear another student talking about Seiji and his experience over the weekend with the local police. Mrs. Mokes asks a few questions and finds out that Seiji had gotten drunk on Saturday night, and upon returning to the residence hall early Sunday morning, hit his resident advisor in the face. The advisor called the police who arrived and took Seiji in for questioning. He returned to the dorm later and was quite ill due to his hangover.

Questions for Discussion

1. What additional information would help you better understand this case?

2. To what extent is Mrs. Mokes' attendance policy fair?

3. To what extent does Seiji have a legitimate excuse for his absence? To what extent is he covering a potentially unexcused absence?

4. What reasons might Seiji have for giving Mrs. Mokes the excuse he did?

5. What issues are involved in Mrs. Mokes' decision to discuss Seiji with another student? What reasons might she have had for doing so?

6. Do you think Seiji's explanation can be considered a lie? Why or why not?

7. What are some ways an instructor might deal with a student who is not completely truthful?

8. What options for dealing with Seiji's situation are available to Mrs. Mokes in this case?

Extending the Case

Consider the two situations presented. Then reflect on these questions: (1) How does each situation differ from or relate to this case? (2) What contributing factors come into play in each situation? and (3) What are the possible courses of action for each?

1. A student from Argentina always arrives at least ten minutes late to class. He enters quietly and takes his seat but then leans over to a neighbor to ask what he has missed. The instructor decides to incorporate a segment into the class about different cultural understandings of time. All of the students find the lesson very interesting and even jokingly mention that the Argentinian obviously has a different cultural understanding of time. He laughs with the others and continues to arrive late to class.

2. A student from Brazil is recruited to play soccer for an American university. His English is weak, and he enrolls in the IEP for his first semester on campus. The athletic department communicates with the program director and states that the student will need to be absent for away games. One of his instructors assigns frequent oral reports and insists that students give them on their assigned day. The Brazilian student has to play in several away games and misses giving several of his oral reports. His grade for the course is in jeopardy.

Questions for Further Reflection

1. What is the importance for adult learners of regular class attendance for language learning?

2. To what extent and in what ways should instructors make allowances in attendance for students' personal problems? For religious concerns? For sanctioned athletic competitions?

3. What is an excused absence? An unexcused absence?

4. How can an instructor determine the legitimacy of absences?

5. How can an instructor deal with students who seem to be less than truthful?

6. To what extent should an instructor make decisions regarding excused and unexcused absences based on a student's previous track record regarding attendance?

7. What are some ways an instructor can handle a situation in which a student is consistently late to class?

8. When a problem such as tardiness arises, it is often wise for the instructor to incorporate the issue into a lesson for the whole class. However, when the lesson seems to have no effect on subsequent student behavior, what other options does the instructor have to deal with a student's tardiness?

9. How might attendance affect course grades differently in IEPs, ESL courses in college, and in adult programs? How important is the distinction between excused and unexcused absences in each of these programs?

10. What are the advantages and disadvantages of having a program-wide policy regarding attendance and punctuality?

Delving Deeper

1. Research different cultural views of time. Become familiar with the terms *polychronic* and *monochronic*. Define each term, and explain how these terms relate to one of the cases.

2. Write up a list of at least ten metaphors in English that have to do with time (e.g., *Time is money; Time flies.*). What might these metaphors suggest about the importance of time in American culture? Share your list and ideas with others.

3. Develop an attendance and punctuality statement for a course syllabus. Identify the type of program and level of the course, as these factors will influence your policy. For example, an adult education policy will probably be quite different from an IEP policy in which faculty must legally account for student absences from class. You may wish to consult course syllabi from classes you have had, examples on the Internet, or others. Discuss and compare your statements with others.

Resources

Hall, E. T. (1959). *The silent language*. Greenwich, CT: Fawcett.

———. (1983). *The dance of life: The other dimension of time*. New York: Doubleday.

Lakoff, G., & Johnson, M. (1980). *Metaphors we live by*. Chicago: University of Chicago Press.

Levine, D. R. (1987). *Beyond language: Intercultural communication for English as a second language*. New York: Prentice Hall.

Resolution to the Featured Case

Mrs. Mokes asked Seiji to meet with her during her office hours. She told Seiji that she had gotten some information about what had happened over the weekend and wanted to know if it was true. Seiji confirmed that it was. Mrs. Mokes then asked him if he thought he had an excusable absence. His response was, "Ah, that is very difficult to say." Mrs. Mokes said that she did not think it was difficult. She said it was not an excusable absence, but that she might show some consideration for his grade if he made good progress with his English for the rest of the semester. She also advised him not to drink.

MY THOUGHTS on the Resolution

Case 10

Student Misunderstandings

Walking to his intermediate grammar class five minutes before class is scheduled to begin, Mr. Stone is surprised to meet one of his students walking away from the classroom. The student, Avika Tarapit from Thailand, asks if class is cancelled. Mr. Stone replies, "No. Today is a review for the midterm." Avika then tells Mr. Stone that, having seen a note on the blackboard about a cancelled class, some of the students told her that class had been cancelled. When Avika and Mr. Stone arrive in the empty classroom, they see there is a note on the blackboard. Evidently the class before had been cancelled. The note, however, clearly, gives the faculty member's name (Ms. Ferguson) and the name of the class, Advanced Speaking. As Mr. Stone sets down his books and Avika takes her seat, a few other students come in, but at the time the class is scheduled to begin fewer than half the students have arrived. Avika says that she saw several students leave because they thought class had been cancelled. Mr. Stone conducts the review for the midterm and states that the exam will be given as scheduled during the next class period.

Questions for Discussion

1. What additional information would help you better understand this case?

2. How do you think Mr. Stone feels about this situation?

3. How do you think Avika and the other students attending the class feel?

4. How do you think the students who left the class, thinking it had been cancelled, feel when they learn that the class met as scheduled?

5. What arguments can be given for having the midterm the next period as planned? For postponing the midterm?

6. How could this situation have been avoided or was it unavoidable? How could similar situations be avoided in the future?

7. What options does Mr. Stone have for dealing with this situation? Evaluate each option.

Extending the Case

*Consider the three situations presented. Then reflect on these questions:
(1) How does each situation differ from or relate to this case? (2) What
contributing factors come into play in each situation? and (3) What are
the possible courses of action for each?*

1. The instructor at a community college notices that a student from
   Ethiopia has submitted the incorrect homework assignment. The
   instructor informs the student that his homework is unacceptable and
   that since homework is not accepted late, he will receive zero for the
   assignment. The student replies that he copied the assignment from
   the blackboard during the last period and is sure that the teacher told
   them to submit the exercises that he did.

2. A shy Asian woman asks to speak to the director of the IEP and informs
   him that her TOEFL® preparation instructor told the students that
   he was participating in a neighborhood clean-up project on Saturday.
   He invited students to participate and said he would give extra credit
   to those who did. He also reminded students of other ways to earn
   extra credit. The student is unsure about what to do and asks for
   advice. She does not want to go but is afraid that her grade will
   be lowered if she does not attend. She asks the director, "Should
   I go?"

3. On their midterm exam, university students are instructed to answer
   10 of 15 short answer questions. The instructions say, "Choose ten
   of the questions below and answer each in a short paragraph. If you
   answer more than ten, only the first ten will be read and graded." A
   Mongolian student has trouble finishing the exam and asks for more
   time. The instructor tells her that her time is up, and she must hand
   in her exam because students in the next class are waiting to enter the
   room, and all her classmates have finished the exam. In grading the
   exams, the instructor discovers that the woman had done all 15 of
   the short answer questions so had been unable to complete the last
   section of the exam.

Questions for Further Reflection

1. What factors may contribute to misunderstandings between faculty and students?

2. What steps can an instructor take to see that students' misunderstandings about assignments, due dates, exams, and other course requirements are minimized?

3. What steps can an instructor take to determine whether students are clear about what is optional for the course (e.g., extra credit or activities that do not influence grades) and what is required?

4. If an instructor feels that he or she is at fault for a student's misunderstanding, what can the instructor do to ameliorate the situation?

5. How do you think an instructor's reaction would differ depending on whether one student misunderstands or if most of the students misunderstand?

6. How can faculty help students develop skills in asking different types of questions (e.g., questions about content, questions for clarification)?

7. What are some ways an instructor might handle student accusations of miscommunication or error in class? Evaluate each response.

8. How is not following directions on an exam different from or the same as not following directions for a homework assignment? Should points be taken off if a student does not follow directions on an exam? On a homework assignment? Should the instructor's response to a student's first misunderstanding be different than the response to a student's repeated misunderstandings?

9. What are some ways that an instructor can help students take responsibility for their own actions and misunderstandings (e.g., not following directions, not turning in work on time, not arriving at an appointed place on time)?

10. How can all students be treated fairly when some misunderstand? For example, what are the possible effects on other students in the class if the instructor does not hold individual students accountable for understanding and following directions?

Delving Deeper

1. Student misunderstandings can be based on culture, language, or both. Culture includes educational practices. Sometimes, English itself is the problem. English modals, in particular, can contribute to misunderstandings in that students are unclear about their meanings in a given context. Find lessons in two grammar books on modal auxiliaries. Compare the definitions and explanations. Can you improve on these definitions and explanations by creating examples and/or sample dialogues? For example, if a definition of one meaning of *must* is *be required to,* you could explain it in more depth by adding, "You have no choice." Select two modals that have similar meanings in certain contexts. Explain the context and make the distinction between the two modals as clear as possible.

2. Speech act theory can help explain discourse and misinterpretations of utterances. From the list below, select one pair of speech acts and explain how the two acts differ from each other. First, focus on the actual linguistic choices a native speaker might use to make the distinction clear. Then indicate how prosody and non-verbal features (e.g., tone of voice, eye contact, intonation, volume) might help listeners discern the intention of the speaker. Also, consider why students, especially non-native English speakers, might misinterpret these types of utterances. Use the Internet and other resources in analyzing these speech act pairs. Write about your ideas to share with your classmates.

   a. a suggestion vs. a directive

   b. an explanation vs. an excuse

   c. a complaint vs. an objection

   d. a complaint vs. a whine

3. Examine each of the situations presented again. Speculate about the extent to which cultural issues and educational experience (as opposed to linguistic issues) might help explain the misunderstandings. Also speculate about the extent to which student carelessness might account for the misunderstandings. Write about your thoughts to share with others.

Resources

Austin, J. L. (1975). *How to do things with words* (2nd ed., J. Urmson & M. Sbisa, Eds.). Cambridge, MA: Harvard University Press.

Celce-Murcia, M., & Olshtain, E. (2000). *Discourse and context in language teaching: A guide for teachers.* New York: Cambridge University Press.

Flaitz, J. (Ed.). (2003). *Understanding your international students: An educational, cultural, and linguistic guide.* Ann Arbor: University of Michigan Press.

———. (2006). *Understanding your refugee and immigrant students: An educational, cultural, and linguistic guide.* Ann Arbor: University of Michigan Press.

Larson-Freeman, D. (2003). *Teaching language: From grammar to grammaring.* Boston: Thomson/Heinle.

Searle, J. R. (1969). *Speech acts.* Cambridge, UK: Cambridge University Press.

Resolution to the Featured Case

After class, Mr. Stone emailed all the students, stating that he understood that some students had felt that class had been cancelled so had left early. He informed students that the note on the blackboard had clearly indicated that the previous class, Ms. Ferguson's, had been cancelled, not his class. He went on to say that the review session for the midterm had been held as planned and that the exam would take place in the next class as scheduled. He also attached his notes from the review session and encouraged students to email him or visit him during office hours with any questions. He closed by saying that students who did not attend class earlier that day would not be counted absent.

MY THOUGHTS **on the Resolution**

Case 11   Class Visitors

Ms. Millhouse has taught for four years at an adult night school program in a local school district. She enjoys teaching and the students like her; they especially enjoy her conversation classes. Occasionally Ms. Millhouse brings her six-year-old daughter to class. Ms. Millhouse and her husband are divorced, and she obtained custody of the couple's six-year-old child, a lovely little girl named Nan. As a result, Ms. Millhouse is not financially well off, and she has a hard time making ends meet. Because of her financial situation, she is reluctant to hire babysitters. Often her sister helps, but from time to time, her sister is not available. Thus, she brings Nan to her conversation class on Tuesday and Thursday evenings from 7:00–8:30, sometimes as often as twice a month. She is able to leave class at exactly 8:30 and therefore feels that Nan will not miss much sleep. In addition, she feels that Nan can occasionally participate in class as another native speaker of English. The students seem to enjoy Nan's presence in class, and they often speak to her. For her part, Nan enjoys coming and she generally colors quietly during class.

One evening, Maria Delgado, a young woman from El Salvador, brings her four- year-old son, Jose. Jose does not sit still during class and talks to his mother in Spanish in a loud voice throughout most of the class.

Questions for Discussion

1. What additional information would help you better understand this case?

2. How do you think the students feel about having Nan in class? About having Jose in class? About having children in class in general?

3. How do you think Ms. Millhouse's supervisor feels about Nan's coming to class?

4. Why do you think Maria Delgado would conclude that it is acceptable to bring Jose to class?

50

5. How do you think Ms. Millhouse feels about Jose coming to class?

6. What do you think Ms. Millhouse could do about Jose's disruptive behavior?

7. What kinds of comments could Ms. Millhouse make to Maria Delgado about bringing her son to class?

8. What are the possible legal implications of Ms. Millhouse's behavior?

9. If you were Ms. Millhouse's supervisor and learned about the children in the classroom, what options would you have for dealing with the situation? What are the advantages and disadvantages of each option?

Extending the Case

Consider the three situations presented. Then reflect on these questions: (1) How does each situation differ from or relate to this case? (2) What contributing factors come into play in each situation? and (3) What are the possible courses of action for each?

1. In her high-level oral communications class, an instructor assigns the students to groups and asks that they each develop a presentation on American teenagers. To help the class with the assignment, she brings her 15-year-old son to class to visit each group so that they can interview him.

2. An instructor brings her small dog, Bruiser, in a portable pen to class a couple of days a week. Bruiser is extremely well-behaved and never barks.

3. A large university has both an IEP and an M.A. TESOL program. Often the M.A. TESOL students observe classes in the IEP. One afternoon, three days before the end of the term, four M.A. TESOL students wait outside the door of the classroom for the IEP instructor to arrive. When he does, they ask if they can observe his class. The instructor says no to the request, explaining that his class is having a practice final that day. The students plead that they must have one more class observation before the end of the semester.

Questions for Further Reflection

1. Have you ever, as a student, taken a visitor to class with you? Describe the situation and how it was handled.

2. Have you ever been a visitor in a class? Describe the situation and how it was handled.

3. List some types of classroom visitors. Which seem appropriate and which seem inappropriate?

4. What are some guidelines for determining appropriate and inappropriate visitors? Who should set these guidelines? What are some advantages and disadvantages of setting program-wide guidelines?

5. Adults often have family obligations that include caring for children. How can institutions assist both students and faculty who have such responsibilities?

6. In the featured case and Item 2 on page 51, is the power differential between faculty and students a factor? Explain your answer.

7. When graduate students need to observe classes as part of a practicum or course requirement, what guidelines need to be in place in order to set up the observation? Whose responsibility is it to set up these guidelines?

8. Have you ever had someone's pet in a classroom or office at a school you were attending? Explain the situation. (*Pet* here does not include an animal assisting a disabled person.)

Delving Deeper

1. Interview at least two faculty members, preferably at different institutions, about their practices and beliefs regarding visitors in class. Write several questions to guide the interview. Possible questions include (a) Does your institution have a policy regarding visitors? (b) Do you have a policy regarding visitors? (c) What do you expect from visitors in the classroom? (d) How do you feel about pets in the classroom? Write about the results of your interviews to share with others.

2. Write a policy statement for inclusion on a syllabus about having and not having visitors in class. Be sure to specify the type of program and level of students. Do you feel that such a statement is warranted on a syllabus? Do you feel that a school or program should have a blanket administrative policy on visitors? Make a list of the issues involved with policies on visitors both in the school and the classroom.

Resources

Hafernik, J. J., & Messerschmitt, D. S. (1994). Fostering cooperation between intensive English programs and teacher education programs. *CATESOL Journal, 7*(2), 103–111.

Resolution to the Featured Case

A student complained to Ms. Millhouse about Jose's presence in the class. The student said that Nan was fine, but Jose was noisy. Ms. Millhouse asked Mrs. Delgado to keep Jose at home but continued to bring Nan. Toward the end of the term the director of the program—who had noticed Nan while walking through the hall—spoke to Ms. Millhouse and told her firmly not to bring her daughter to class.

MY THOUGHTS on the Resolution

Case 12 Third Party Involvement

Jiao Feng, 24, is an international student from the People's Republic of China (PRC) completing her master's degree in public health from a large land grant university. She wants to remain in the United States for an extra year under the U.S. Immigration and Customs Enforcement's Practical Training provisions, and she needs a letter of support from her advisor. Her advisor, Dr. Queens, is a respected scholar in the field of public health. Although Jiao has always had a cordial relationship with him, she does not know Dr. Queens very well; she has taken only one class with him and is one of his many advisees. Actually, she is a little afraid of him. After much thought, she asks a good friend, Jim Hu, a Chinese American student, to approach Dr. Queens with her request for a letter of support for practical training in the United States.

Jim Hu, who barely knows Dr. Queens, visits him during his office hours and explains Jiao's situation. Jim concludes by asking Dr. Queens to write a letter of support for Jiao's application for practical training in the United States. Dr. Queens is taken aback by the request and tries to remember details about Jiao. He vaguely recalls Jiao and wonders why she has not made the request herself. Dr. Queens politely explains to Jim that Jiao needs to make her request directly to him. When Jim meets Jiao later that day for coffee and tells her of his meeting with Dr. Queens, she is quite surprised and disappointed that he has not been able to obtain the letter of support that she needs.

Questions for Discussion

1. What additional information would help you better understand this case?

2. Why do you think Jiao asked her friend Jim to make her request to Dr. Queens?

3. How do you think Dr. Queens views Jim's visit and his request? Do you think he considers it impolite? How do you think the use of a go-between would be considered in the PRC?

4. How might Jiao view Dr. Queens' response?

5. Think of two or three scenarios of what might happen next in this situation. Explain why you think each scenario is possible, and identify one you think most likely. Be prepared to explain your reasoning.

6. What different cultural norms does this case illustrate?

Extending the Case

Consider the four situations presented. Then reflect on these questions: (1) How does each situation differ from or relate to this case? (2) What contributing factors come into play in each situation? and (3) What are the possible courses of action for each?

1. When a Taiwanese student arrives for her scheduled appointment with her instructor to discuss her most recent essay, her U.S. boyfriend is with her. The woman explains that she has asked her boyfriend to come to take notes and to help her understand the professor's advice.

2. A faculty member receives an email from the wife of an Indian student in his graduate ESL class, asking for clarification of a homework assignment for her husband. The professor has never met the student's wife.

3. The research papers for a community college writing class are due by 5:00 PM and the faculty member has repeatedly said that she will not accept late papers. During her office hours that afternoon, a male student from Ecuador, whom she has never met, visits her office. He explains that his partner is in her writing course, and he has come to submit his partner's research paper.

4. An Indonesian student withdraws from an IEP early in the program and returns home. Several weeks later, his former roommate visits the director of the program. The roommate indicates that the Indonesian student wants a refund from the program and requests that the school send the check to Indonesia. The former roommate asks what he needs to do to get the refund.

Questions for Further Reflection

1. How would you define go-betweens or third parties?

2. What function do go-betweens, in general, serve?

3. Have you ever used a go-between? If so, please explain the situation.

4. Give some examples of situations in the United States when using a go-between is not possible.

5. When are go-betweens typically used in the United States? In U.S. academic situations?

6. In the United States, what role do instructors expect friends and family to play in a student's academic work?

7. What are examples of country/cultural differences between the U.S. and other countries/cultures with regard to the role of friends and families in students' interactions with instructors? In academic work?

8. In the examples you listed for Question 7, which cause few or no problems for U.S. faculty? Which examples might cause problems for U.S. faculty? Explain your answers.

9. What responsibility do faculty members have to help students understand what is generally considered an appropriate use of go-betweens in the U.S. academic community?

10. How, if at all, is networking similar to using a go-between?

Delving Deeper

1. A term that has become more common in recent years is *helicopter parents*. What does this term mean, and how is it generally used, especially with regard to academic situations? Do you think the actions of *helicopter parents* or similar behaviors are common in other countries and cultures as well as in the U.S.? Provide specific examples of actions by helicopter parents. Look for recent articles and websites about this phenomenon to help you answer these questions. Write about what you find and be prepared to share your findings with others. Document your sources.

2. Go-betweens are used in non-academic situations in certain cultures (e.g., in arranging marriages, in business and political negotiations). Lewis (2006, pp. 167–169) says that in some cultures, such as Japan and China, the use of go-betweens (i.e., middle-persons) is acceptable and valued in negotiations and in compromises, whereas their use is less acceptable in Western cultures. List specific examples of the use of go-betweens in non-academic contexts and the cultures and/or countries where these situations can be found. How are these situations similar to and different from academic situations? Make a chart of your findings.

Resources

Family Educational Rights and Privacy Act (Buckley Amendment). www.epic. org/privacy/education/ferpa.html.

Flaitz, J. (Ed.). (2003). *Understanding your international students: An educational, cultural, and linguistic guide.* Ann Arbor: University of Michigan Press.

————. (2006). *Understanding your refugee and immigrant students: An educational, cultural, and linguistic guide.* Ann Arbor: University of Michigan Press.

Lewis, R. D. (2006). *When cultures collide: Leading across cultures* (3rd ed.). Boston: Nicholas Brealey.

Resolution to the Featured Case

Jiao felt that Dr. Queens did not want to write her a letter of support since he had refused Jim's request. She decided to ask another professor for a letter instead. For his part, Dr. Queens was puzzled by the whole situation. He looked up Jiao's record and realized that she had done well in her classes. He decided that he would agree to write her a letter of support if she asked him.

MY THOUGHTS on the Resolution

Case 13

Student Attire, Hygiene, and Mannerisms

Ms. Presno and Mr. Riordan both teach the low-intermediate class at an IEP at a rural community college. The class is small with only ten students, three women and seven men, all under the age of 25. One day in the faculty room during lunchtime, Mr. Riordan and Ms. Presno begin talking about the low-intermediate class and its students. Mr. Riordan is particularly concerned about one student, Tatyana Yelinson, an attractive 19-year-old woman from Belarus. Mr. Riordan comments on Tatyana's beauty, her mannerisms, and her attire, pointing out that she wears high heels, short tight skirts, low-cut blouses, jewelry, and heavy makeup. He adds that her appearance and mannerisms often seem distracting to the male students, who have trouble keeping their eyes off her during class. Mr. Riordan is more concerned, however, that outside of class Tatyana may be inviting unwanted attention because of the way she dresses and carries herself. Mr. Riordan then asks Ms. Presno to speak to Tatyana and to explain how her manner of dress may be perceived by others. Mr. Riordan would like Ms. Presno to encourage Tatyana to wear what he terms "more appropriate" clothing and to suggest she flirt less with men. Mr. Riordan adds that he thinks it would be inappropriate for him or any male to discuss Tatyana's physical appearance and behavior with her and that these suggestions would be better coming from a female instructor. He argues that he only has Tatyana's best interests in mind by making this request.

Questions for Discussion

1. What additional information would help you better understand this case?

2. Do Mr. Riordan's comments and observations about Tatyana's behavior and choice of attire seem appropriate? Do you think he would make similar comments about a male student? Explain your answer.

3. Is the faculty room, as opposed to a more public space, a more appropriate place for the conversation about a student between two faculty members?

59

4. How do you think Tatyana's attire and mannerisms might impact classroom dynamics?

5. How do you think Ms. Presno feels about Mr. Riordan's language in describing Tatyana? About his request?

6. Does Mr. Riordan's request seem appropriate?

7. Does Mr. Riordan's argument that a female and not a male should discuss these issues with Tatyana seem convincing? Why or why not?

8. How do you think Tatyana would react if Ms. Presno spoke to her about her attire and mannerisms?

9. What options does Ms. Presno have in responding to Mr. Riordan's request? Evaluate each option.

Extending the Case

Consider the three situations presented. Then reflect on these questions: (1) How does each situation differ from or relate to this case? (2) What contributing factors come into play in each situation? and (3) What are the possible courses of action for each?

1. A course for newly admitted graduate students at a large land grant university is designed to acculturate international students to the U.S. graduate academic community as well as help them improve their speaking and writing skills. Early in the semester, the instructor notices that two of the male students, one from the Middle East and one from Latin America, have noticeable body odor, yet they sometimes wear strong aftershave. The instructor is about to begin a unit on interactions between students, faculty, and others in the U.S. academic community. One area of discussion will be levels of formality expected in various situations. She wonders if she can bring in the idea of hygiene and personal appearance but worries about offending her students.

2. The instructor of an adult ESL literacy class notices that a middle-aged Romanian man in the class likes to talk to and flirt with his young female classmates before and after class and sometimes even during class. He sometimes comments on their appearance and clothing. Several of the young women joke and flirt with him, whereas others seem unsure about how to respond to his attentions. Several of the

older women have commented to the instructor that the Romanian's behavior is "bad." The instructor fears the man's flirting may be making some of the women uncomfortable.

3. One day in a beginning-level listening class, students are practicing asking Yes/No questions and *wh-* questions, using advertising flyers from a local department store. A young man from South America asks his classmate, a young Muslim woman, "Why do you always wear a headscarf? Do you like to wear a headscarf?" The woman seems embarrassed by the questions and the young man's attention to her attire.

Questions for Further Reflection

1. When, if at all, does student attire negatively impact the classroom and learning?

2. Think of some situations in which a student's mannerisms and/or hygiene could positively or negatively impact the classroom and learning environment. Can you think of examples from your own experience?

3. Have you ever attended a school that required uniforms? One that had a dress code? If yes, describe how the requirement that students wear uniforms or abide by a dress code impacted the learning environment.

4. How might school uniforms and dress codes for students in the United States and in other countries differ? For example, are uniforms more common in elementary and high schools in other countries than in the United States? Give specific examples from your own experience, if possible, or ask friends about their experiences.

5. What factors does an instructor need to consider in deciding whether to bring up a topic related to attire, hygiene, or personal mannerisms with an individual student? With the whole class?

6. How can an instructor respond if a student brings up a sensitive and/or personal subject such as hygiene, attire, or sex in class? In private?

7. How does the make-up of a group, including the instructor, impact discussions on sensitive topics? For example, does it matter if the class is largely male or female and the instructor is male when discussing issues related to dating, hygiene, or attire?

8. How might the culture of a student impact a teacher's decision to discuss or not discuss a certain topic with a student of the opposite sex?

9. How can faculty help students understand common expectations and perceptions regarding attire, mannerism, and hygiene in the United States, especially in U.S. academic settings?

Delving Deeper

1. Cultural attitudes about personal mannerisms, attire, behavior, and hygiene (e.g., burping, sneezing, coughing, slurping, snapping of fingers, body odor, hair growth) vary widely. Select two countries that you are familiar with, or investigate them through the use of resources, to find out more about different attitudes. (You may wish to focus on two or three items.) Write about your findings and be prepared to share them with others.

2. Attire varies greatly in the United States, as well as in other countries, depending on numerous factors (e.g., setting, age, and occupation). Look at the list of fashions, and comment on how common and appropriate each seems: (a) for college students in the U.S., (b) for college students in another country or countries (pick specific countries with which you are familiar), (c) for faculty in the U.S., and (d) for faculty in another country or countries (pick specific countries with which you are familiar).

blue jeans	suit and tie (men)	tattoos
T-shirts with slogans	suit (women)	body piercing
brightly dyed hair (e.g., orange, blue, purple, green)	baseball caps or hats	shorts
	sunglasses	sweatshirt hoods
slacks (women)	flip-flops or sandals	pajamas
low-cut blouses (women)	heavy makeup	nail polish
jewelry (men & women)	gym or exercise clothes	long hair (men)

Resources

Flaitz, J. (Ed.). (2003). *Understanding your international students: An educational, cultural, and linguistic guide.* Ann Arbor: University of Michigan Press.

————. (2006). *Understanding your refugee and immigrant students: An educational, cultural and linguistic guide.* Ann Arbor: University of Michigan Press.

Lewis, R. D. (2006). *When cultures collide: Leading across cultures* (3rd ed.). Boston: Nicholas Brealey.

Resolution to the Featured Case

Ms. Presno listened politely to Mr. Riordan but found his description and characterization of Tatyana troublesome and offensive. She told him that she would consider his request; she readily agreed that it would be awkward and possibly perceived as rude for him to speak to Tatyana directly about his concerns. During the next few class periods, Ms. Presno paid attention to how the other students, especially the men, reacted to and interacted with Tatyana. While she noticed that the male students did look at Tatyana frequently, she did not feel Tatyana's attire or behavior were negatively impacting class. In fact, she noticed that many U.S. women dressed more provocatively than Tatyana did. Therefore, she decided not to speak to Tatyana. Neither she nor Mr. Riordan brought up the subject of Tatyana's attire and mannerisms again.

MY THOUGHTS on the Resolution

Case 14   Student Disabilities and Mental Health

The week before classes are to begin, Ms. Geraci receives a telephone call and follow-up email from Disability Services at the university where she teaches. The disability officer informs her that a student in her composition course is hearing impaired. The student, Ekber Suleymanoglu from Turkey, will be provided with a note-taker and a transcriber who will record everything said in the class. Ms. Geraci is told that Ekber reads lips fairly well but does not know sign language or speak clearly. The semester begins and other students are friendly and helpful to Ekber, yet he still seems isolated in class, without any real friends. It is difficult for him to actively participate in class discussion as everything that is said and that he says must be transcribed. Also, group work is cumbersome in that any group he is in has two extra people, Ekber's note-taker and transcriber, who seem to create a physical barrier between Ekber and the other students. Ms. Geraci finds that Ekber needs extra attention to understand directions for assignments, and conferencing with him on papers proves time-consuming. It is difficult for her to distinguish between Ekber's linguistic problems and problems created by his disability. Ms. Geraci consults with the disability officer, receives helpful information and advice, but is still not sure how to make Ekber fit into the class better and how to best teach Ekber without taking attention away from other students.

Questions for Discussion

1. What additional information would help you better understand the case?

2. How do you think Ekber feels about his academic situation (i.e., needing special accommodations)?

3. How do you think Ms. Geraci feels about having Ekber in the class?

4. How do you think the other students feel about Ekber and about having him in class?

5. What strategies can Ms. Geraci use for working with Ekber's note-taker and transcriber?

6. What strategies can Ms. Geraci employ to help other students accept Ekber as an equal member of the class?

7. What are some strategies Ms. Geraci can use to help Ekber become just another student in the class? Is this a desirable goal?

Extending the Case

Consider the three situations presented. Then reflect on these questions: (1) How does each situation differ from or relate to this case? (2) What contributing factors come into play in each situation? and (3) What are the possible courses of action for each party involved in the situation?

1. An instructor is concerned about the health of a young woman from Colombia in her community college class. The student is extremely thin, seems listless at times, and overall does not look healthy. She is very attractive and seems concerned about how she looks, often applying makeup in class and generally wearing the latest fashions. The instructor asks some of her other colleagues if they have also noticed the girl's unhealthy appearance. They agree that the student looks anorexic. All are concerned about her health but aren't sure what to do.

2. Shortly after the semester begins at a rural college, a Norwegian student comes to the office of his TOEFL®-preparation course instructor to give her a form from the Disability Services office on campus indicating that he is entitled to receive special accommodations, specifically extra time for exams. The student tells the instructor that he is dyslexic and works very slowly. The form indicates that the Disability Services office will administer any tests for the class and asks the instructor to answer several logistical questions. She says that she will complete the form as requested and is willing to help him be successful in the class. After the student leaves, she wonders how his dyslexia will affect his ability to do in-class activities such as reading aloud and doing timed exercises. She does not want to draw attention to him and his disability but is unsure about what to do.

3. After several class periods of an IEP integrated skills course, the faculty member asks an Israeli student to speak to him in his office. He explains that he is concerned about her because some of her classroom

behaviors are inappropriate and unacceptable. For example, she sometimes walks up to him and asks a question while he is speaking to the
class as a whole. Sometimes she is attentive and focused, and at other
times she seems distracted, asking her neighbors questions unrelated
to the lesson or staring out the windows, her thoughts seemingly
miles away. She also has outbursts of laughing or crying. Sometimes
she begins talking quickly, and at times her meaning is hard to follow.
She confides that she has bipolar disorder and has recently switched
to a new medication. She adds that some days she feels fine, and on
those days she does not take her medication.

Questions for Further Reflection

1. List three to six types of student learning and physical disabilities (e.g.,
   dyslexia, quadriplegia). How might a student with these disabilities
   impact a class? A school environment?

2. List two or three types of student mental health disabilities or issues
   (e.g., eating disorders, paranoia) that may be present in a class. How
   might a student with these disabilities impact a class? A school environment?

3. Physical disabilities are usually visibly evident but other types may not
   be. What actions can faculty take if they suspect that a student has a
   learning disability? A mental health disability?

4. In and out of class, how can faculty not draw attention to or embarrass
   a student who has a disability?

5. What can faculty do to maintain student confidentiality with regard
   to disabilities?

6. Who should know about a student's disabilities or mental health issues?
   The student's teachers? The program director? Other faculty?

7. What strategies can faculty use to help students with disabilities or
   mental health issues, acknowledged or not, be a part of the class as
   much as other students?

8. Does it seem appropriate for faculty to take any disability into consideration when grading student work and assigning grades? Explain
   your answer.

9. How can faculty respond if a student says that he or she has a disability but has not gone through the appropriate channels to be legally designated as having a disability?

10. What strategies can faculty use to develop awareness and tolerance among students and faculty for individuals with disabilities in general?

Delving Deeper

1. Look at your list of student disabilities and student mental health issues in Questions 1 and 2 (Questions for Further Reflection). Select one or two to research. You may wish to contact a Disabilities Service office or advisor on a school campus or use the Internet and other resources. Find clear definitions and learn what an individual must do to be legally considered disabled. Find out what types of accommodations the American Disabilities Act of 1990 requires for the disability (disabilities) you selected. Write about your results and be ready to share your findings with others. Document your sources appropriately.

2. Through research or interviews with individuals from other countries, learn about how other countries view, treat, and accommodate individuals with disabilities or mental health problems. For example, in the United States, sidewalks can accommodate individuals in wheelchairs as do public transportation systems. Select one or two countries as your focus. You may also wish to limit your research to one or two disabilities, perhaps those you chose for Activity 1. Write about your results and be prepared to share your findings with others. Document your sources appropriately.

Resources

Americans with Disabilities Act: ADA. www.ada.gov.

Healthy Minds/Healthy Bodies. www.healthyminds.org/collegementalhealth.cfm.

Kadison, R., & DiGeronimo, T. F. (2004). *College of the overwhelmed: The campus mental health crisis and what to do about it.* San Francisco: Jossey-Bass.

Koslow, D. R., & Salett, E. P. (1989). *Crossing cultures in mental health.* Washington, DC: SIETAR International.

Mooney, J., & Cole, D. (2000). *Learning outside the lines: Two Ivy League students with learning disabilities and ADHD give you the tools for academic success and educational revolution.* New York: Fireside.

National Eating Disorders Association. www.nationaleatingdisorders.org.

National Institute of Mental Health. www.nimh.nih.gov.

Shulman, D. (2002). Diagnosing learning disabilities in community college culturally and linguistically diverse students. *Journal of Postsecondary Education and Disability, 16*(1), 17–31.

Resolution to the Featured Case

Ms. Geraci struggled all semester with how to help Ekber be a successful member of her class. She worked closely with Disability Services and with Ekber's note-taker and transcriber. However, Ekber never seemed to connect with his classmates or interact with them outside of class. He had trouble following directions and meeting deadlines. He was, in fact, one of the weakest writers in the class. He earned a C and went on to the next course.

MY THOUGHTS on the Resolution

Case 15 Risky Behaviors

Hilda Morales from Mexico arrives early to school one morning so that she can talk to Mr. Jack Bloom, the director of the IEP. When Mr. Bloom is told of Hilda's request, he comes to the reception area, greets Hilda, and asks her to follow him into his office. Mr. Bloom senses that Hilda is anxious, so he tries to put her at ease by asking her how she is and briefly talking about the weather. When he asks her why she wanted to speak to him, Hilda begins to talk haltingly but becomes more relaxed as she continues. Hilda explains that she thinks that Mr. Joe Maxwell, her grammar teacher, is picking on a classmate, Makiko Suzuki, from Japan, because Makiko smokes. Hilda says that Mr. Maxwell often writes sentences on the board about Makiko's smoking. For example, when practicing the past continuous tense, he has written "Makiko was smoking during the break." In addition, he has said that Makiko will die sooner than the other students because she smokes. Hilda notes that Makiko never complains and even smiles and laughs quietly, but Hilda thinks that everyone in the class is uncomfortable when Mr. Maxwell draws attention to Makiko's habit of smoking. Even though Hilda agrees that smoking is unhealthy, she feels sad for Makiko.

Question for Discussion

1. What additional information would help you better understand this case?

2. How can Mr. Bloom verify the validity of Hilda's statements?

3. How do you think Hilda feels before and during her conversation with Mr. Bloom?

4. How do you think Hilda views Mr. Maxwell's treatment of Makiko, her classmate?

5. Assuming that Hilda's comments are accurate, how do you think Makiko interprets Mr. Maxwell's actions? How do you think Mr. Maxwell justifies his actions toward Makiko?

6. How can Mr. Bloom make Hilda feel more comfortable during their conversation?

7. How do you think Mr. Bloom views the information that Hilda gives him?

8. How do you think Mr. Bloom interprets Hilda's statement that "Everyone in the class agrees with me"?

9. When talking to Hilda, what responsibility, if any, does Mr. Bloom have to defend Mr. Maxwell when he hears of Hilda's concerns?

10. What options for responding to Hilda does Mr. Bloom have? Evaluate each option.

Extending the Case

Consider the three situations presented. Then reflect on these questions: (1) How does each situation differ from or relate to this case? (2) What contributing factors come into play in each situation? and (3) What are the possible courses of action for each?

1. A faculty committee is preparing a study skills workshop to be presented to all students. They agree to include statements in a PowerPoint® presentation and handout that urge students to get enough sleep, eat a healthy diet, and exercise. One faculty member strongly feels that they should also include a statement such as "Do not drink alcohol, smoke, or have unprotected sex." Some others feel uncomfortable with such a direct statement because all students are adults and most are over age 21, some much older.

2. An instructor invites a guest speaker from the community to speak to her adult immigrant students on the topic of HIV/AIDS during class time. She does follow-up language work in the next three class periods, spending much time on preventive measures such as practicing safe sex and using clean needles for intravenous drugs. An older Russian woman complains to the instructor's supervisor that talking about sex and drug use makes her uncomfortable. She adds that some of the advice is against her religious beliefs and that the material is inappropriate. She argues that she enrolled to learn English, not about issues related to sex and drugs.

3. An instructor notices that a young male student from Hong Kong always seems tired and sleepy in her 10:30 AM class. Also, he seldom submits his homework on time and, when he does, it is obviously hastily done. She speaks to him after class one day, expressing her concerns for his well-being and his performance in class. He says that he stays up very late and, therefore, has trouble waking up in the morning and staying alert in class. When asked what he does into the early hours of the morning, he replies that after seeing ads for several gambling sites on a social networking site, he began playing Texas Hold 'Em online. Now he loves to play every night. When questioned about his online gambling losses, he says that he has lost money, more than he will tell his parents about, but he is sure that he will win big soon. He feels lucky. As a second thought, he adds that he will try to be a better student.

Questions for Further Reflection

1. To what extent is it appropriate for an instructor to draw public attention to students who engage in healthy behaviors and/or to those who engage in risky behaviors?

2. List examples of risky behaviors that college-age and adult students might practice.

3. How do views and definitions of risky behavior vary from culture to culture?

4. How do views and definitions of risky behavior vary depending on the gender of the person practicing the behavior? In the U.S.? In other cultures?

5. To what extent do ESL instructors have a responsibility to educate students about the dangers of risky behaviors (e.g., drugs, smoking, unprotected sex, Internet addiction, not wearing seat belts)?

6. Should faculty consider cultural taboos (e.g., against talking about sex with mixed gender groups) both before and while discussing certain subjects with students? If so, how can they do this?

7. Give examples of specific ways that faculty can address risky behaviors and healthy behaviors in the ESL curriculum and classes (e.g., in reading selections).

8. Draw up some guidelines for addressing risky behaviors with sensitivity to and respect for differences in students' cultural and religious beliefs, gender, and so on.

Delving Deeper

1. Select a risky behavior (e.g., substance abuse, Internet addiction, not wearing a seat belt when in a car). Define and research the behavior, using resources to find out more about it (e.g., prevalence, symptoms, preventive measures). Develop an introductory lesson on the topic. Use a lesson plan format, with several different activities and documented resources. First, specify the English level of the students and the type of learning environment. What vocabulary, idioms, and grammatical points need to be included? What types of content material can be used (e.g., readings, video clips, news articles)?

2. Many universities now require students to complete an alcohol and drug education course during their first year on campus. The course is generally online, so students can complete it at any time. Additionally, many campuses have groups for individuals recovering from addictions (e.g., Alcoholics Anonymous). Research an institution that you have attended or are familiar with to discover what type of alcohol, drug, and similar educational programs and support the institution provides for students, especially those for students who have exhibited risky behaviors in the past. Is the information targeted to individuals who are not native speakers of English or those from different cultural or ethnic groups? If not, how might the information be improved to better target these individuals? Be prepared to share and discuss your findings, either in written or oral form.

Resources

Centers for Disease Control and Prevention/College Health. www.cdc.gov/Features/CollegeHealth.

4College Women—Health. Our Way. www.4collegewomen.org.

Kadison, R., & DiGeronimo, T. F. (2004). *College of the overwhelmed: The campus mental health crisis and what to do about it.* San Francisco: Jossey-Bass.

National Center on Addiction and Substance Abuse. www.casacolumbia.org.

National Council on Problem Gambling. www.ncpgambling.org.

Resolution to the Featured Case

Mr. Bloom listened carefully to Hilda and understood her concerns. He stated that he knew Mr. Maxwell cared about each student personally and was concerned about each student's health. Mr. Bloom stated that he felt that Mr. Maxwell's intentions were good. He said that he would speak to Mr. Maxwell about the situation. Hilda asked that her name not be used. Mr. Bloom assured her that he wouldn't use any student's name.

Later that day, he spoke to Mr. Maxwell privately and told him that some students in his class felt that he was picking on Makiko because she smoked. Mr. Maxwell confirmed that he did comment on her smoking to the class as a whole. Mr. Maxwell then began talking about the harmfulness of smoking. He added that he never meant to embarrass or ridicule any student, especially not Makiko. Mr. Bloom agreed that smoking was a bad habit, but he asked that Mr. Maxwell consider how best to help students understand the dangers of smoking while at the same time respecting each student and not embarrassing them. Mr. Maxwell said he would be more cautious in the future.

MY THOUGHTS on the Resolution

Case 16 Stress

Tai Li, from Taiwan, is a quiet 23-year-old first-year graduate student in chemistry at a large university. He was admitted to the chemistry department on the condition that he enroll in a graduate-level speaking and writing class in the ESL Department in order to improve his English competence.

Ms. Vaughn, Tai Li's ESL instructor, observes that Tai has seemed uninterested in his ESL class from the first day. She suspects he is more interested in chemistry than in English. He attends class regularly but does the minimum amount of work. His written work is marginal, and he speaks in class only when called on. As the semester progresses, Ms. Vaughn observes that Tai seems even less interested in her class, and his behavior changes. Sometimes he is late for class, or he does not come at all. In class, he often falls asleep. Homework assignments arrive late or not at all. One day after class, Ms. Vaughn asks Tai if everything is alright. He blurts out, "No, I'm doing badly chemistry." Ms. Vaughn probes further. "What do you mean? What are your grades so far?" Tai replied that he had received a B on his midterm. He then said, "My father is going to yell at me if I don't get an A. I can't sleep at night, and I just can't eat anything here."

Questions for Discussion

1. What additional information would help you better understand this case?

2. What are some possible sources of Tai's stress?

3. What issues do you think Ms. Vaughn could discuss with Tai? How should she prioritize these issues?

4. What institutional resources do you think would benefit Tai? At what point, if any, should Ms. Vaughn recommend these resources to Tai?

74

5. How much consideration should Ms. Vaughn give to Tai's concerns and fears about his performance in his chemistry class when grading him for her class?

6. If you were Ms. Vaughn, what advice would you give Tai? Address each issue listed in your answer to Question 3.

Extending the Case

Consider the three situations presented. Then reflect on these questions: (1) How does each situation differ from or relate to this case? (2) What contributing factors come into play in each situation? and (3) What are the possible courses of action for each?

1. A Catholic priest from the Democratic Republic of Congo (DRC) is studying TESOL methodology classes in the United States as a special student for one semester. He plans to return home to teach English at a private school for boys. In the course of the semester, there are several newspaper reports of strife in his homeland. However, he never mentions anything about the situation and keeps up well with his classwork. One day after the report of a particularly brutal incident in the DRC, several students approach the instructor and ask her what they can do to support their classmate. At lunch, he had confided to them that he was very worried about his mother and father back in Africa.

2. By chance, an adult education instructor meets one of her Hispanic students in the local grocery store. The student is frequently absent, and other students have told the instructor that the woman is having personal problems. During the instructor's conversation with the student at the store, the woman begins to cry and confides that she is having problems with her teenage daughter and that her husband has lost his job.

3. An instructor notices that a Croatian woman is tired in class and often turns in work that seems hastily done. In speaking to the student after class one day, the instructor learns that she works as a clerk at a department store in the mall 30 hours a week while taking a full load of courses. The student says that she often does not have as much time as she'd like to study.

Questions for Further Reflection

1. List three or four types of stress that students may experience.

2. What kinds of stresses do you think adult learners and college-aged ESL learners have in common? Which of these stresses might be different for each?

3. To what extent should faculty members ask students about stressors in their lives?

4. What are some ways a faculty member can help students cope with stress?

5. When a student is experiencing stress-related issues or crises, at what point should a faculty member step back and refer students to skilled professionals in counseling?

6. What kinds of institutional and community resources are available to students experiencing stress in their lives?

7. Does it seem appropriate for faculty to offer advice to students about making changes in their lives so that they are less stressed (e.g., working fewer hours, dropping some classes)?

8. To what extent, if at all, should faculty members take student stress into account when evaluating students?

Delving Deeper

1. Interview an international or immigrant student about stress. What types of stress has the student experienced? To what extent are these the everyday stresses of academic work? To what extent are the student's stresses different from the usual academic worries of most students? What, if anything, has the interviewee done to handle these stresses? Write about your findings and be prepared to share them with others.

2. Write a description of what you would do to assist the student you interviewed. If the student you interviewed seems to have only everyday stress, identify some of the usual ways students in the U.S. deal with it. Do you think these coping mechanisms would be helpful to international and immigrant students as well?

Resources

Coffee, M., & Grace, S. (1997). *Intercultural advising in English-language programs*. Washington, DC: NAFSA.

Family Educational Rights and Privacy Act (FERPA). www.ed.gov/policy/gen/guid/fpco/ferpa/index.html.

Greenblatt, S. (1999). Advising students facing a political crisis at home. *International Educator, 8*, 23–26, 52.

Greenblatt, S., & Rose, J. K. (2001). Advising students facing political and financial crises back home. In P. A. Burak & W. W. Hoffa (Eds.), *Crisis management in a cross cultural setting* (Rev. ed.), (pp. 43–55). Washington, DC: NAFSA.

Kadison, R., & DiGeronimo, F. T. (2004). *College of the overwhelmed: The campus mental health crisis and what to do about it*. San Francisco: Jossey-Bass.

Scollon, R., & Scollon, S. B. K. (1983). Face in interethnic communication. In J. C. Richards & R. W. Schmidt (Eds.), *Language & communication* (pp. 156–188). New York: Longman.

Vandrick, S. (1997). The role of hidden identities in the postsecondary ESL classroom. *TESOL Quarterly, 31*, 153–157.

Resolution to the Featured Case

Ms. Vaughn spoke to Tai Li at length about his situation and the grading system in the United States, explaining that a B is not a bad grade. She told him about the counseling services available on campus. She observed that his behavior in class did not change, and she calculated his grade at B minus for his English course. She never found out his final grade in the chemistry course.

MY THOUGHTS **on the Resolution**

Case 17

Religious Beliefs and Practices

In a university oral communications course, students give speeches regularly and often must lead one discussion on a controversial issue during the semester. Students choose interesting topics, and discussions are generally lively. The class is multicultural, with students from Asia, Scandinavia, the Middle East, and South and Central America. This semester the class also includes a Catholic priest from Mexico. One particularly heated discussion centers on world population. It begins when a student from the People's Republic of China explains China's one-child policy. At one point during the discussion, Raul Mendoza from Ecuador speaks about poor families in his country who have large families, blaming the Catholic Church and the priests in the villages for encouraging couples to have more children and telling them that it is against God's will to use birth control. He stresses that he has seen these poor families and witnessed their struggles, and he has heard priests tell them to continue to have children. Raul argues that it is immoral for priests to take such a position, because the parents live in poverty and cannot feed and clothe the children they have. He argues that the priests say this only to increase the number of Catholic parishioners and do not care that the parents struggle to support their families. How, he asks, can priests and the Church be so heartless and do such deliberate harm to those they say they are helping? The classroom is completely quiet because it is obvious how strongly and sincerely Raul feels about this issue. Ms. Eisenstein, the instructor, feels the tension in the air and wonders what Father Chavez from Mexico is thinking.

Questions for Discussion

1. What additional information would help you better understand this case?

2. How do you think Raul feels? On what belief system does he base his argument? How do you think Raul feels while he is speaking?

3. How do you think Father Chavez feels about Raul's comments?

4. How do you think Ms. Eisenstein and the other students in the class feel at this point?

5. What options does Father Chavez have at this point in the discussion? What are the advantages and disadvantages of each option?

6. What options does Ms. Eisenstein have at this point in the discussion? What are the advantages and disadvantages of each option?

Extending the Case

Consider the three situations presented. Then reflect on these questions: (1) How does each situation differ from or relate to this case? (2) What contributing factors come into play in each situation? and (3) What are the possible courses of action for each?

1. In a proprietary intensive English school in a downtown office building in a large city, writing instructors often have students keep weekly journals. In one journal, a quiet Taiwanese woman writes that she has recently joined a Bible study group that meets twice a week. She explains that she was invited by an American man she met downtown, outside of the building. She continues, "I am not a Christian, and I know very little about the Bible. I go to the Bible study group to practice my English. Everyone is very nice, and I am becoming friends with the man who initially invited me."

2. The principal for the adult school that holds classes during the day and evening receives several complaints from students and faculty about standing water in the men's restroom. Individuals say that standing water on the floor and the general untidiness of men's restrooms creates an unsanitary environment that makes others hesitant to use the restrooms. Upon investigation, she discovers that the Muslim men in her class wash themselves in the basins in the restrooms before praying.

3. Several Muslim students come to the director of a program and ask if the college can provide a place for the Muslim students to pray. They ask to be excused from class on Friday afternoons so that they can pray. Later the same day, Catholic students ask the program director if they can be excused the following Wednesday so that they can attend Mass on Ash Wednesday.

Questions for Further Reflection

1. What are some reasons for including discussions of controversial topics in an ESL class? Are there reasons for avoiding such topics? Are there any topics that could be considered completely off limits? If so, give some examples.

2. If an instructor chooses to include controversial topics in class, what are some ways to promote healthy disagreement?

3. What are the advantages and disadvantages of discussing religion and religious issues in class? Of presenting the subject and issues explicitly? Of allowing discussions that simply arise?

4. In what ways can knowing something about the religious backgrounds of students positively impact an instructor's teaching and classroom practices? Try to identify specific benefits.

5. What are some of the arguments for and against allowing students to miss class for religious reasons?

6. What kinds of accommodations seem appropriate for students who make special requests because of their religious beliefs?

7. How can an instructor know if students are sincere in their requests for accommodations for religious purposes and not simply using their religious commitments as an excuse? If an instructor suspects a student is not sincere in his or her request, what can the instructor do?

8. What kind of explanation to students is warranted when other students receive special treatment due to religious reasons? For example, if Muslim students are allowed to miss Friday afternoon classes so that they can pray, what, if anything, is appropriate for the faculty member to say about this situation to other students?

9. What are the advantages and disadvantages of having a program-wide policy concerning accommodations for religious reasons?

10. A person's religious beliefs are a very personal matter. What are some ways for faculty to respect an individual student's privacy when religious issues are introduced in class?

11. Faculty, like students, may have strongly held religious beliefs. What seems appropriate for faculty to reveal about their own religious beliefs?

12. How can faculty promote religious understanding and tolerance among students?

Delving Deeper

1. Interview someone who has a religious faith different from yours. Before interviewing the person, research the religion to gather basic information. There are numerous websites that explain the religions of the world. Good keywords or descriptors are *world religions* and *religions of the world*. Write several questions to begin your interview, for example, What are several principles on which your religion is based? Who are important individuals in your religion? What are the most important religious holidays? How are they celebrated? Write about your findings and be prepared to explain them to others.

2. Historically, there have been conflicts about religion. Select a movie that portrays the conflict between different religions or religious beliefs. What values are in conflict in the movie you select? Watch the movie, and then write a short summary discussing the values in conflict, as well as a short plot summary. Some movies that focus on religious conflicts include *The Mission, The Messenger, Shogun, Black Robe, A Man for All Seasons*, and *The Boxer*.

Resources

Edge, J. (2003). Imperial troopers and servants of the Lord: A vision of TESOL for the 21ˢᵗ century. *TESOL Quarterly, 37*, 701–708.

Internet Movie Database (IMDb). www.imdb.com.

Ishi, S., Klopf, D., & Cooke, P. (2009). Worldview in intercultural communication: A religio-cosmological approach. In L.A. Samovar, R. E. Porter, & E. R. McDaniel (Eds.), *Intercultural communication: A reader* (12ᵗʰ ed.), (pp. 28–36). Boston: Wadsworth Cengage Learning.

Smith, H. (1991). *The world's religions: Our great wisdom traditions* (2ⁿᵈ ed.). New York: HarperCollins.

Varghese, M. M., & Johnston, B. (2007). Evangelical Christians and English language teaching. *TESOL Quarterly, 41*, 5–31.

Resolution to the Featured Case

Father Chavez listened intently to Raul and when he finished, Father Chavez acknowledged the poverty in many Latin American countries and agreed that families often have so many children that they cannot adequately provide for them. He also acknowledged Raul's passionate feelings, asserting that Raul's position is legitimate. He tactfully neither defended the priests and the Catholic Church nor blamed them. His comments were spoken with sincerity and calmness, easing the tension in the air. Ms. Eisenstein thanked Raul, Father Chavez, and others for their thoughtful comments. Fortunately, there was little class time left, so she reminded students of upcoming assignments and the speakers for the next class period. Then she dismissed the class.

MY THOUGHTS **on the Resolution**

Case 18 Discrimination

Mr. Tomkins is committed to helping his multilingual writers matriculate into the first-year composition class at a midsize urban university. He works hard to create interesting and challenging writing assignments that will prepare students not only for writing classes but also for classes in other subjects where they have to write essays, essay exams, and research papers. One assignment that he and the students seem to always enjoy is based on primary research. Mr. Tomkins spends several class periods explaining what type of primary research students can do and has students brainstorm and discuss possible projects. Students have to do an interview, survey, or observation. Most students choose to interview one to three people or do a survey of more than 20 people. Mr. Tomkins suggests that students give him a draft of their interview questions or survey before conducting their research; however, he does not insist that they do so.

Henry Chang, recently arrived from Peru, is enthusiastic about the research project and decides to survey international students and native speakers about their leisure activities. He is interested in learning if the two groups spend their free time in similar ways. Henry is an eager, talkative student who tends to make negative comments about his own abilities and work. For example, when handing in an essay he often remarks, "I didn't do very well on this. I think I will get a bad grade." Despite his lack of self-confidence, Henry's papers are always thoughtful, creative, and well-organized. Admittedly, his papers generally have numerous sentence-level errors but few that make comprehension difficult.

One day before class, Mr. Tomkins asks Henry how his research is going; Henry has not shown Mr. Tomkins a draft of his survey. Henry states that he is disappointed that he has only 20 of 50 surveys returned. He had slipped the surveys under doors in his residence hall, giving his room number and name and asking individuals to return them to him. He says that he has received one survey from a native speaker that upsets him. He hands the survey to Mr. Tomkins, asking him to read the comments written in large letters in bold, red ink: "Why are you asking these stupid questions? You are wasting my time. This is full of errors. You shouldn't be in college. You don't know English. You need to go back to your country."

83

Questions for Discussion

1. What additional information would help you better understand this case?

2. Do the native speaker's comments on Henry's survey constitute discrimination? If so, what type of discrimination?

3. How do you think Mr. Tomkins views the incident? How do you think he feels when Henry relates the incident to him?

4. How do you think Henry feels about the incident? In what ways could Henry explain the incident to himself?

5. What steps can Mr. Tomkins take to help Henry understand the incident? To help Henry feel less hurt by the comments written on the survey?

6. What responsibility, if any, does Mr. Tomkins have to report the incident to university officials? With Henry's consent? Without Henry's consent?

7. If Mr. Tomkins decides to report this incident to others, does he need to inform Henry and keep him abreast of further developments?

8. What actions can Mr. Tomkins take to minimize these types of situations in the future?

Extending the Case

Consider the three situations presented. Then reflect on these questions: (1) How does each situation differ from or relate to this case? (2) What contributing factors come into play in each situation? and (3) What are the possible courses of action for each?

1. A Brazilian student tells his community college instructor that a group of U.S. students in the school cafeteria called him "a fag." He asks what that means.

2. While walking down the hall to class, an instructor hears a U.S. student shout angrily at a student from Malaysia, " You m__ f__. What are you grinning about? Don't you ever do that again!"

3. After class one day, a Japanese student asks to speak to her instructor, who is also a woman. She explains that in her U.S. history class, the male professor often makes remarks that make her feel uncomfortable, such as, "Asian women are naturally quiet and don't like to talk in class." Or, "Asian women are beautiful, sexy, and make good lovers." She isn't sure what to do and asks for advice.

Questions for Further Reflection

1. Develop a working definition of *discrimination* in a U.S. context. List several examples of discrimination.

2. Develop a working definition of *hate crime*.

3. What are some ways that an instructor can help students understand what constitutes discrimination in the United States?

4. What are some ways that an instructor can help students understand their legal rights with regard to discrimination?

5. How can an instructor help a student who has been the object of discriminatory verbal comments? Of a hate crime? In each case (i.e., discrimination and hate crimes), what are the instructor's responsibilities to the student? To the institution?

6. What are some sources of advice and assistance for a faculty member who becomes aware of an incident of discrimination against a student? An incident that has traumatized a student?

7. What are some sources of advice and assistance for students who feel they may have suffered discrimination?

8. What are some considerations regarding confidentiality with regard to the individual who feels discriminated against? With regard to the individual accused of discriminating against another individual?

9. Imagine that a student has experienced an incident of discrimination and informs one of his or her instructors, who then informs the IEP director. The institution is now investigating the incident. The student is so traumatized that his or her classwork is affected. Which of the following individuals has a need to know about the incident? To whom should the IEP director explain the situation? Does the severity of the incident impact the needs-to-know provision? Explain your answers.

   a. the student's instructors

   b. the student's classmates

   c. the student's academic advisor

   d. the student's roommate or partner

   e. the student's parents

10. What are some ways for faculty and students to work to reduce or eliminate discrimination in classrooms? On campus? In the community?

11. Students sometimes ask about discrimination in the United States. How can an instructor respond in a thoughtful way?

Delving Deeper

1. Discrimination may be perceived and defined differently in different countries and cultures and by different individuals. Additionally, each educational institution has specific definitions of and procedures for dealing with alleged incidents of discrimination. These definitions and procedures comply with U.S. laws and regulations. Research published definitions of discrimination and procedures for handling alleged incidents of discrimination at a post-secondary educational institution, perhaps one you have attended or where you have worked. Often institutions have this information on their website and in student handbooks, in print and online. Write about your findings in a chart or an essay. Indicate the name and place of the institution and document your sources appropriately.

2. Find definitions for the term *stereotype* on the Internet or in print publications. What are common stereotypes associated with Americans? Write a short explanation of at least three of these stereotypes. Why do you think these stereotypes developed and still persist? What are the dangers of stereotyping?

3. Research the minority groups that exist in at least two other countries. To what extent do members of these groups face discrimination? How does this discrimination manifest itself? Summarize your findings and be prepared to discuss them with others.

Resources

Kadison, R., & DiGeronimo, T. F. (2004). *College of the overwhelmed: The campus mental health crisis and what to do about it.* San Francisco: Jossey-Bass.

Kappra, R., & Vandrick, S. (2006). Silenced voices speak: Queer ESL students recount their experiences. *CATESOL Journal, 18*(1), 138–150.

Murray, D. (Ed.). (1992). *Diversity as resource: Redefining cultural literacy.* Alexandria, VA: TESOL.

Samovar, L. A., & Porter, R. E. (2001). Accepting and appreciating similarities: A point of view. In L. A. Samovar & R. E. Porter, *Communication between cultures* (4th ed.), (pp. 263–303). Belmont, CA: Wadsworth/Thomson.

Schniedewind, N., & Davidson, E. (2000). Linguicism. In M. Adams, W. J. Blumenfeld, R. Castaneda, H. W. Hackman, M. L. Peters, & X. Zuniga (Eds.), *Readings for diversity and social justice* (pp. 19–20). New York: Routledge.

Vandrick, S. (1997). The role of hidden identities in the postsecondary ESL classroom. *TESOL Quarterly, 31,* 153–157.

Resolution to the Featured Case

Mr. Tomkins was surprised and saddened by the comments written on the survey that Henry showed him. He noticed that there were several grammatical and spelling errors in Henry's survey, but the directions and questions were all comprehensible. Mr. Tomkins told Henry that there were a few minor errors on the survey, but that it was a good survey and an interesting topic. He added that the return rate of 40 percent was actually good, so he should be pleased. When Mr. Tomkins asked Henry about other survey responses, he said that these comments were the only negative ones he received. Mr. Tomkins said that the individual who wrote these comments was rude to have responded the way he or she did. Mr. Tomkins added that, unfortunately, some individuals did not understand or appreciate the contributions Henry and other international students were making to the institution or how much they were accomplishing by studying in English, their second or third language. In fact, he added, discrimination against individuals from other cultures and countries happens in the United States, even on university campuses. Mr. Tomkins urged Henry not to be discouraged or hurt by the comments. He assured him that he was a good student and could be successful in his academic studies. He ended the conversation by asking if Henry would like to speak to a counselor about this incident and he invited him to talk to him about this or other matters at any time.

MY THOUGHTS **on the Resolution**

Case 19

Technology and Modern Life

In a class for new international graduate students at a large university, students are required to lead a class discussion. Mr. Ronald McKenny guides them in preparing for the activity. Each discussion is videotaped, then put up on the class website in the campus course management system. After viewing the discussion online, students must evaluate their presentation as well as their participation in the discussions. As required, in preparation for his discussion in the next class period, Jozef Stevecky from the Slovak Republic provides his classmates with an article about the American character. The article highlights individualism, the value placed on freedom of speech, and the belief in free markets and capitalism. In introducing his topic before the discussion, the student cautions his classmates to recognize that individual Americans and the U.S. government are distinct. The discussion is lively, with students expressing agreement and disagreement with the author's arguments as well as comments about the situation, people, and governments of their own countries. Strong political statements are made as are heartfelt criticisms of specific government policies including those of the United States and other countries. One student, Hai Nguyen from Vietnam, is particularly vocal in his criticism. At the end of the class, after the video technician who films the discussions has left, Hai admits to the instructor and his classmates that he feels uncomfortable about having comments he made during the discussion posted on the course website and available on the Internet. He hesitantly asks the instructor what can be done.

Questions for Discussion

1. What additional information would help you better understand this case?

2. Why do you think Hai feels uncomfortable about being videotaped? About having his comments made public on the course management system and the Internet?

3. How important is it for students to become accustomed to being filmed and videotaped?

4. What are the advantages and disadvantages of having student presentations videotaped and requiring students to critique their own work?

5. What options does Mr. McKenny have in response to Hai's request? How does each option affect Hai and Jozef?

Extending the Case

Consider the three situations presented. Then reflect on these questions: (1) How does each situation differ from or relate to this case? (2) What contributing factors come into play in each situation? and (3) What are possible courses of action for each?

1. During the application process for a new student from Tonga, his sponsor asks if the IEP can provide the student with basic typing and computer skills as well as English courses. The student's English is advanced, and he has been accepted into a graduate program in theology for the next semester. However, he has no computer skills, which he will need for his graduate studies.

2. An instructor of a vocabulary and idioms class utilizes a course management system such as Blackboard® for her class. The class is completely paperless, except for the textbooks. Any handouts, exercises, or practice sheets are put on the course website and students must submit all work electronically. The class meets only once a week for three hours, so the instructor uses the class time for discussion and oral activities with the targeted vocabulary and idioms. Each week students are required to do several things online: (a) take a quiz, (b) submit original sentences using the new words and idioms, and (c) do a crossword puzzle or other word-game activity. In the first class, the instructor helps students enroll online and explains clearly what is expected. One student is erratic in submitting her work and frequently asks for hard copies of material. The instructor explains that the course is paperless and she will not give handouts of the material that is online. Several weeks into the semester, when the instructor asks the student about her failure to submit work, the student replies that her computer is very old, her Internet connections at home are very slow, and her password doesn't seem to work, so she frequently does not have access to the course. She adds that she hates computers. She repeats her request for hard copies of everything that is online.

3. A large urban adult school district has a technology bus that goes from campus to campus offering ESL and basic computer skills courses and holding open hours for students to use the computers and other technology. When the technology bus is on a campus, child care is also provided for adults who wish to take the computer classes or utilize the computers during open hours. The instructor is pleased that several Hispanic women return each week for the computer class, though initially they find computers intimidating. In fact, one woman tells him, "I'm so glad that I can use a computer. It helps me with my English. My husband doesn't have computer skills and doesn't really like my learning to use them or attending these classes." Shortly after their conversation, one morning in class around 11:30, the woman receives a phone call from her husband. After the call, she tells the instructor that she must go get her daughter from daycare and return home to prepare lunch for her husband. The instructor says, "I hope you return next week," to which the student replies, "I don't know. I must ask my husband."

Questions for Further Reflection

1. What kinds of political climates in a student's home country could affect his or her willingness to be videotaped?

2. What cultural and personal factors, as opposed to political climates, could affect whether a student feels comfortable being taped?

3. What do you think is the range of students' comfort level with computers and other technology?

4. If only one student in a class is unfamiliar with using technology, what are some options for providing the individual with assistance?

5. If students do not have good, convenient access to technology in their current living situations, what are some options for them?

6. What obligations does an instructor have to provide alternatives to students who do not have or who are not comfortable using technology to do the required coursework? Do the available options depend upon the type of institution at which a student is enrolled (e.g., university, community college, adult school)?

7. How can instructors utilize the expertise of students who are competent and well-versed in using technology in their classes to make other students more computer literate and comfortable with technology?

8. Is it important for faculty to use technology in language teaching? Explain your answer.

9. What kinds of language content and skills seem to lend themselves to the use of technology (e.g., for practice)? Which ones seem less suited to technological application?

10. How can faculty stay abreast of advances in using technology in the classroom? How can they develop new skills?

Delving Deeper

1. Make a list of new developments in the use of technology in classrooms (e.g., podcasts, clickers, blogs, skype, wikis, social networking). Using the Internet and other resources, select two or three technologies and explain how each can be used to enhance language learning. Give specific examples of activities using these technologies that would be appropriate for language classrooms. Write about your findings and be ready to discuss them with others. Be sure to document your sources appropriately.

2. Using the list of new developments in technology you generated in Activity 1, make a chart following the template presented. Interview several faculty members to complete the chart.

Technology	Have Used? Yes/No	If Yes, how? Give one specific example.	Advantages of Using This Technology	Advice about Using This Technology
MP3 program (e.g., Audacity® or QuickTime®)				

Resources

Chapelle, C.A. (Ed.). (2000). TESOL in the 21ˢᵗ century [Special issue]. *TESOL Quarterly, 34,* 3.

Egbert, J. (2005). *CALL Essentials: Principles and practices in CALL classrooms.* Alexandria, VA: TESOL.

Egbert, J., & Hanson-Smith, E. (Eds.). (1999). *CALL environments: Research, practice, and critical issues.* Alexandria, VA: TESOL.

Murray, D. (2000). Protean communication: The language of computer-mediated communication. *TESOL Quarterly, 34,* 397–421.

Warschauer, M. (2000). *Electronic literacies: Language, culture, and power in online education.* Mahwah, NJ: Lawrence Erlbaum.

Resolution to the Featured Case

The instructor understood Hai's concerns about having his comments on the course website. As a class, the students discussed Hai's concerns and the options available. The instructor asked Jozef if he would consent to his discussion not being posted on the course website. The instructor explained that he could do his self-evaluation based on his memory of the discussion since he would not be able to watch it. The instructor assured Jozef that his grade would not be affected. Jozef agreed to not having his discussion posted. The instructor told Hai and the other students that she would immediately contact the appropriate individuals and tell them not to put Jozef's discussion on the website. After class, that is what she did, and the tape of Jozef's presentation was destroyed.

MY THOUGHTS on the Resolution

Case 20 Cheating

Charles Kim, a Korean graduate student in an M.A. TESOL degree program, discusses the topic of his final thesis project with his advisor, Dr. Moeller, early in his program. Students are expected to check in with their advisor several times during the semester and present a prospectus for approval. Charles, a very popular young man with a good command of English, decides to investigate the history of English language teaching in Korea. Dr. Moeller approves of the topic and expects to be updated with progress reports from time to time. Charles, however, never appears, never turns in a prospectus, and when the final thesis is due, leaves it in the instructor's mailbox. The topic of the paper is "Discrimination against Koreans in Japan." Dr. Moeller is quite surprised, since both the topic and the student's behavior seem out of character. On a hunch that something may be wrong, she contacts Dr. Sanchez, Charles' Sociolinguistics instructor. She finds out that Charles is an excellent student who makes good contributions to class discussions. In fact, his oral report on discrimination against Koreans in Japan was excellent. Dr. Moeller is now suspicious, and she and Dr. Sanchez continue to talk. Dr. Moeller learns that in Charles' Sociolinguistics course, the final paper is based on the oral report. Therefore, she and Dr. Sanchez agree to confer after Charles turns in his final paper for Sociolinguistics. When he does, it turns out that the two papers are exactly the same, word for word, although the final thesis project contains one extra section to make it longer.

Questions for Discussion

1. What additional information would help you better understand this case?

2. Why do you think Charles turned in the same paper for two different classes?

3. Why do you think Charles avoided contacting Dr. Moeller earlier in the semester?

4. What could Dr. Moeller have done earlier to perhaps avoid the situation that developed?

5. How do you think Dr. Moeller feels about this situation?

6. How do you think Dr. Sanchez feels about this situation?

7. How do you think Charles feels about using the same paper for two different courses?

8. What is a possible first step for Dr. Moeller to take in dealing with Charles now?

9. What actions, if any, could Dr. Sanchez take?

10. What are some possible consequences for Charles' behavior? What are the advantages and disadvantages of each?

11. When and to what extent does it seem appropriate for either instructor to inform the administration of what has happened? What kind of documentation seems appropriate?

Extending the Case

Consider the three situations presented. Then reflect on these questions: (1) How does each situation differ from or relate to this case? (2) What contributing factors come into play in each situation? and (3) What are the possible courses of action for each?

1. During an in-class quiz on irregular past tense verb forms, a student from Mexico sitting in the back row appears to be using a cheat sheet. The instructor walks closer to the student, who quickly shoves something into his pocket.

2. When correcting an essay exam, an instructor notices that two papers are exactly the same. Therefore, she gives both students a grade of F for the test and keeps the papers. Shortly after grades are posted, both students independently make appointments to see the instructor, claiming not to understand the failing grade. Each student claims that it was the other one who must have copied.

3. About an hour before their ten o'clock math class, a female international student often studies in the coffee shop with an American man in her class. At first they simply compare answers on the homework, but as the semester progresses the American shows up later and later with no homework and begins to simply copy her answers. She feels uncomfortable with the situation but is unsure about what to do. She asks her ESL instructor for advice.

Questions for Further Reflection

1. Define cheating.

2. What do you think is the usual definition of cheating in a U.S. academic environment?

3. Is the definition of cheating absolute? What are some gray areas?

4. What do students need to know about cheating?

5. What are some possible cultural differences in students' understandings of cheating?

6. How are cheating and plagiarism different? Give some examples of each.

7. How proactive should an instructor be in looking out for instances of cheating?

8. When does it seem appropriate to report an instance of cheating to an administrator? Give specific examples.

9. What can an instructor do to minimize cheating on classwork and tests?

10. How important is it for an instructor to obtain and keep evidence of cheating behaviors?

11. What are some possible consequences of cheating?

12. What responsibility do instructors have to explain to students the definition of cheating and the consequences of such behavior?

13. What is an institutional honor code? Find an example of an institutional honor code. What are the advantages and disadvantages of an honor code? A good place to find this information is on the Center for Academic Integrity website under "Codes and Policies."

Delving Deeper

1. Develop a vocabulary lesson that is appropriate for the topic of cheating. That is, think of vocabulary that is used when discussing cheating in English. How would you teach these concepts? Identify the level of the students and the teaching situation, for example, low-level adult or intermediate-intensive English.

2. Educational systems vary from country to country. Within each educational system, what is considered "sharing with a friend" and what is considered "cheating" may differ. For example, in *Understanding Your International Students: An Educational, Cultural, and Linguistic Guide* (2003), Flaitz writes about the student-student relationship in Saudi Arabia. "Relationships between students are close and noncompetitive. Cheating is often regarded as sharing or helping a friend or a brother" (p. 133). Similarly, in describing Russian-speaking students' views of helping others, Malko writes, "Russian-speaking students' attitude toward cheating is less negative because refusal to allow another student to copy from their papers can be perceived as a selfish, unfriendly action and in extreme cases may lead to ostracism by the peers" (2006, p. 129). Consult Flaitz's books, Malko's article, or other sources for information about how cheating is viewed in three different cultures and educational systems. Present your findings in a chart, and be prepared to compare your findings with others. If you know individuals from the countries you research, ask them if they agree with your findings.

3. Search for articles about academic integrity in one of the sources listed in the Resources. A good place to begin is the Center for Academic Integrity website under Educational Resources. Find an article that addresses one or more of the questions or issues raised in this case, or one that interests you. Write a summary of and reaction to the article, and be prepared to explain the article to others. Use appropriate documentation.

Resources

Center for Academic Integrity. www.academicintegrity.org.

Flaitz, J. (Ed.). (2003). *Understanding your international students: An educational, cultural, and linguistic guide.* Ann Arbor: University of Michigan Press.

———. (2006). *Understanding your refugee and immigrant students: An educational, cultural, and linguistic guide.* Ann Arbor: University of Michigan Press.

Hafernik, J. J., Messerschmitt, D. S., & Vandrick, S. (2002). Cheating and plagiarism. In *Ethical issues for ESL faculty: Social justice in practice* (pp. 41–49). Mahwah, NJ: Lawrence Erlbaum.

Kuehn, P., Stanwyck, D. J., & Holland, C .L. (1990). Attitudes toward "cheating" behaviors in the ESL classroom. *TESOL Quarterly, 24,* 313–317.

Malko, V. A. (2006). A comparative analysis of American and Russian ESL/EFL classroom cultures. *CATESOL Journal 18*(1), 122–137.

Smith, P. (1994). Cheating in the ESOL classroom: A student-centered solution. *TESOL Journal, 4,* 51.

Resolution to the Featured Case

Dr. Moeller called Charles to her office and presented him with both papers. Charles said very little. Dr. Moeller told him she could not accept his work. He asked if he could get his degree. Dr. Moeller said no. She said she planned to speak to the dean and advised Charles to see him as well. She later took the papers to the dean and left them with him, telling him that she would not work with Charles in the future. The dean called Charles in and the two worked out a plan with another professor to complete a project on a different topic. About four months, later Dr. Moeller learned that Charles never completed the alternative project and left the United States, thus never finishing his degree.

MY THOUGHTS on the Resolution

Case 21 Plagiarism

Professor Weinstein supervises the field project experience for the students in the M.A. TESOL program at a small university. The field project involves developing an original teaching module in the field. The module must be supported by a short review of related literature. The final product is a paper with two parts: the short literature review and the module development.

There are many international students in the program, most of whom generally plan to return home to teach English. One student, Wei Lin from Taiwan, needs to return to Taiwan early and asks if she can mail in her paper on the topic of vocabulary development for Taiwanese elementary school children. Professor Weinstein consents since she had already approved the topic.

When Professor Weinstein receives the paper, it is grammatically perfect. In fact, it is too perfect, so Professor Weinstein decides to check on the work by inserting several strings of words from the paper into an Internet search engine. She immediately finds several documents with wording that exactly matches the wording on Wei Lin's paper. In addition, source references cited in the Internet articles match the references at the end of Wei Lin's paper. It is clear that Wei Lin has simply taken all of her information from Internet sources and copied much of it word for word. She did not correctly document any of her sources.

Questions for Discussion

1. What additional information would help you better understand this case?

2. To what extent is what Wei Lin has done considered plagiarism?

3. Do you think cultural differences could explain her actions?

4. Do you think Wei Lin felt that she was plagiarizing?

5. How do you think Professor Weinstein feels about this situation?

6. How could Professor Weinstein possibly lessen the likelihood of this situation occurring in the future?

7. What options does Professor Weinstein have for dealing with the present situation? What are the advantages and disadvantages of each option?

Extending the Case

Consider the two situations presented. Then reflect on these questions: (1) How does each situation differ from or relate to this case? (2) What contributing factors come into play in each situation? and (3) What are the possible courses of action for each?

1. A Cambodian student submits a short paper with neither in-text citations nor a reference list but includes photocopies of the sources themselves. In reading the paper, the instructor finds that the student has copied directly and extensively from these sources without using quotation marks or citations appropriately.

2. A Middle Eastern student submits an essay that is much better than his previous work. The instructor speaks to him about the improvement, and he informs his instructor that his girlfriend, who is from the U.S., helped him with his paper but that the ideas are all his. He reminds the instructor that she had suggested that students get a friend to read over their papers or go for help at the Writing Center on campus.

Questions for Further Reflection

1. What factors should an instructor consider when deciding whether or not to allow a student to complete work *in absentia*?

2. Give a definition of academic integrity that would be generally accepted in U.S. academe.

3. What are some possible differences in cultural understandings of academic integrity?

4. Think of a situation that would clearly be considered plagiarism in a U.S. academic setting and one that is not as clear. For example, how much and what kind of help from a friend is inappropriate?

5. What are the advantages and disadvantages of an instructor's use of programs that detect plagiarism?

6. In what ways can instructors help students understand what constitutes plagiarism in the Western academic tradition?

7. What can instructors do to reduce the likelihood of students plagiarizing essays or other written work? Give some examples.

8. What is cyber-plagiarism, and how does it differ from other types of plagiarism?

9. List and evaluate some ways that faculty can handle first instances of plagiarism. What should they do when there are repeated offenses?

10. Find out if an institution that you are associated with or know of has a policy on plagiarism and cheating. If so, what is it? A good place to look is the Center for Academic Integrity website under "Codes and Policies."

Delving Deeper

1. Assume that you are in charge of purchasing a plagiarism identification program for your institution. Browse the Internet for several examples. Then list three or four and develop a template of features to help you decide which one to purchase. For example, you could include price and ease of use. Make your choice and list your reasons.

2. Appropriate referencing is a feature of the Western academic tradition. Not all cultures require the same level of rigor in this regard. Thus, bibliographic concepts can be difficult to teach. Develop an introductory lesson for students on the kinds of information that should and should not be referenced. This should not be a lesson on how to cite sources correctly but, rather, to give students a con-

ceptual framework for evaluating what does and does not need to be referenced. In developing this conceptual framework, you may wish to consult handbooks or Internet sites such as Purdue University's Online Writing Lab (OWL) and articles on the Center for Academic Integrity website.

3. Search for articles about cyber-plagiarism or plagiarism in general on one of the websites listed under Resources. Write a short summary and reflection, with appropriate documentation. Be prepared to explain and lead a discussion on your chosen article.

Resources

Braine, G., & May, C. (1996). *Writing from sources: A guide for ESL students.* Mountain View, CA: Mayfield.

Center for Academic Integrity. www.academicintegrity.org/index.php.

Guide to Plagiarism and Cyber-Plagiarism. library.ualberta.ca/guides/plagiarism.

Hacker, D. (2003). *Rules for writers & working with sources.* Boston: Bedford/St. Martins.

Hacker, D., & Fister, B. (2006). *A writer's reference & MLA quick reference card.* Boston: Bedford/St. Martins.

Hafernik, J. J., Messerschmitt, D. S., & Vandrick, S. (2002). Cheating and plagiarism. In *Ethical issues for ESL faculty: Social justice in practice* (pp. 41–49). Mahwah, NJ: Lawrence Erlbaum.

Harris, R. (2001). *The plagiarism handbook: Strategies for preventing, detecting, and dealing with plagiarism.* Los Angeles: Pyrczak.

Lunsford, A. A. (2006). *Easy writer* (3rd ed.). Boston: Bedford/St. Martins.

Pennycook, A. (1996). Borrowing others' words: Text, ownership, memory, and plagiarism. *TESOL Quarterly, 30,* 201–230.

Pennycook, A., Chandrasoma, R., & Thomson, C. (2004). Beyond plagiarism: Transgressive and nontransgressive intertextuality. *Journal of Language, Identity and Education 3*(3), 171–193.

Plagiarized.com: The Definitive Guide to Internet Plagiarism. www.plagiarized.com/index.html.

Purdue University Online Writing Lab (OWL). http://owl.english.purdue.edu.

Raimes, A. (2008). *Keys for writers* (5th ed.). Boston: Houghton Mifflin.

Resolution to the Featured Case

Professor Weinstein emailed Wei Lin and told her that her project was not acceptable due to her extensive use of Internet sources without appropriate documentation. She referred Wei Lin to the syllabus and a handout she had given her explaining documentation for the project. She allowed her to rework the project, and Wei Lin handed it in one year later. The documentation had improved a bit, although there were still many problems. Professor Weinstein decided that Wei Lin had done an adequate job on the work and gave her a passing grade. Wei Lin finally graduated.

MY THOUGHTS **on the Resolution**

Case 22 Assigning Course Grades

Mr. Wilson has taught composition at the local community college for more than 15 years. He loves his work and enjoys reading his students' papers. He makes the students work hard, gives them much individual attention, and is conscientious. The college has a strict policy that students have to earn at least a C to go to the next writing class, freshman composition. Mr. Wilson allows students who get less than a B on any essay to rewrite it and resubmit it for a higher grade. As the end of the semester approaches, Mr. Wilson encourages all the students to do this by the deadline. One semester, Mr. Wilson is particularly concerned about Peter Lee from China, the most creative and original writer in the class. Peter's writing has a clear voice, insight into difficult issues, and a poetic use of language. Despite this, his writing does display numerous sentence-level errors, so he seldom gets high marks on his essays. Peter has perfect attendance and has visited Mr. Wilson several times during his office hours to discuss his essays. Mr. Wilson is worried about Peter's grade, however, because Peter seldom speaks in class, has failed to turn in all the assigned essays, and has done poorly on some in-class tasks. In fact, on one in-class essay, Peter sat in class staring at his paper for an hour and wrote only two sentences.

The last week of class after the deadline for submitting rewrites, Peter visits Mr. Wilson and explains that he suffers from writer's block and has trouble writing under time constraints. He acknowledges that he failed to turn in several of the assignments and did not rewrite any of his essays as allowed. He asks Mr. Wilson to take his personal writing difficulties into consideration when calculating his course grade and to understand why he has performed as poorly as he has. He goes on to say how important it is for him to receive at least a C in the class and how much he has learned in the class. He assures Mr. Wilson that he is capable of handling the next writing class.

Questions for Discussion

1. What additional information would help you better understand this case?

2. How do you think Peter feels about writing in general? About the class?

3. How do you think Mr. Wilson feels about this situation?

4. How do you think Mr. Wilson could help Peter with his apparent writer's block?

5. How much weight should Mr. Wilson give to Peter's creativity and individual voice in writing? Peter's English accuracy? His completion of work? His visiting Mr. Wilson during office hours for assistance with his essays?

6. What responsibility does Mr. Wilson have to faculty and students in the first-year composition class to ensure that his students are ready for the class and capable of doing the work?

7. What options does Mr. Wilson have in this situation? Evaluate each option.

Extending the Case

Consider the three situations presented. Then reflect on these questions: (1) How does each situation differ from or relate to this case? (2) What contributing factors come into play in each situation? and (3) What are the possible courses of action for each?

1. An Indonesian university student who is on academic probation comes to his instructor and tells her that he needs to get a B in the class or he will be dismissed from the school and be required to return to his country. He says that he is working hard and needs good grades. He says that she is his only hope and pleads for the instructor not to flunk him out of school. Just before leaving, he says that he has a small gift for the instructor and hands her a tasteful expensive handbag and silk scarf.

2. A Peruvian student visits her former writing instructor and asks her to reevaluate her grade from last semester. She was a good student and received an A–. The student explains that if she has a slightly higher grade point average (GPA), she will be able to get a scholarship for next semester. If the instructor would change her grade in the writing class to an A, she would have the required GPA to get the scholarship.

3. A Taiwanese student who took the advanced grammar class last semester comes to his former teacher's office. The instructor is surprised to see the student because he received an F in the grammar class. The student explains that he was having personal problems last semester and, as a result, could not attend class and devote his attention to the class. He asks for a retroactive withdrawal from the grammar course and hands the instructor the form to sign.

Questions for Further Reflection

1. In calculating course grades, what options do faculty members have in weighing performance and effort? What percentage of the total grade seems appropriate for each (i.e., which should count more)? Does the answer to this question depend upon the educational context? For example, should effort count more in adult school classes and performance more at the college level?

2. What obligation do faculty members have to inform students of how grades are calculated? How can faculty provide students with this information?

3. How much flexibility should faculty have in calculating course grades (i.e., should faculty be able to deviate from the published criteria)?

4. What amount of consideration in calculating course grades seems appropriate for students' personal issues and problems (e.g., physical and mental health issues, work obligations, economic pressures)?

5. What role seems appropriate for a faculty member to play in counseling students who exhibit difficulties such as writer's block or experience stress when working under pressure?

6. Many institutions have strict guidelines for assigning an I, or incomplete, as the grade. Under what circumstances does giving an incomplete for a course seem appropriate? What responsibility does a faculty member have to verify an individual student's justifications for receiving an incomplete?

7. Give examples of circumstances under which it seems appropriate for an instructor to reconsider a course grade assigned for a previous semester's course.

8. What responsibility do instructors have to uphold program-wide standards in calculating and assigning grades? For example, many ESL courses act as gatekeepers, determining when students are ready to progress to a more advanced class. How do individual faculty members' decisions impact other faculty and students in future classes?

9. If a program-wide or university standard seems unrealistic, what can a faculty member do with regard to grading individual students? With regard to changing the system?

10. What are the differences between a bribe and a gift?

11. What are examples of gifts that seem appropriate for a faculty member to accept from a student?

12. How is timing important when considering the appropriateness of accepting a student gift?

13. How can a faculty member or program supervisor politely refuse a gift that seems inappropriate due to its excessive value or the particular time or circumstance it is offered?

14. What are the advantages and disadvantages of a program-wide ban on students giving gifts to faculty members?

15. Share your experiences in giving gifts to faculty as a student and in receiving gifts from your own students as an instructor. Listen to others' experiences. In each instance, what seem to be appropriate responses and behaviors on the part of the instructor?

Delving Deeper

1. Collect two syllabi for language courses. Syllabi may be available on the Internet or you may find sample syllabi at institutions with which you are familiar. Examine the grading criteria and how course grades are calculated. Compare and contrast the two syllabi. What are some similarities and differences? Write about your findings. Comment on the appropriateness of the criteria and of the weight (e.g., percentage) given to each component of the total grade. Include the two syllabi with your written work.

2. Gift-giving practices vary across cultures. Research the gift-giving practices of one or two foreign countries and compare them to gift giving in your country. Good resources are books written for business professionals as well as Internet sources. Try searching for "gift giving around the world" or "gift giving for business." Write about your findings or share them orally. Document your sources appropriately.

Resources

Clarke, M. A. (2003). *A place to stand: Essays for educators in troubled times.* Ann Arbor: University of Michigan Press.

Kadison, R., & DiGeronimo, T. F. (2004). *College of the overwhelmed: The campus mental health crisis and what to do about it.* San Francisco: Jossey-Bass.

Messerschmitt, D. S., Hafernik, J. J., & Vandrick, S. (1997). Culture, ethics, scripts, and gifts. *TESOL Journal* 7(2): 11–14.

Morrison, T., Conaway, W. A., & Borden, G. A. (1994). *Kiss, bow or shake hands: Doing business around the world.* Holbrook, MA: Bob Adams.

Resolution to the Featured Case

When Mr. Wilson calculated the course grades, Peter had an average of 62 on his essays, exams, and homework. Ten percent of the grade was for participation, effort, and improvement, so Peter could have an average as high as 72. After much thought, Mr. Wilson assigned Peter a C in the course, an average of 72. Other students who had 72–76 were also given a C and students with averages of 68–72 were assigned a C-.

MY THOUGHTS **on the Resolution**

Case 23   High-Stakes Testing

Keiko Kumadai is a bright, successful Japanese businesswoman in her late twenties. Unlike many of her male counterparts in the company, she has an intermediate-level command of English and can carry on a conversation with native speakers. Because of this, her degree from a prestigious Japanese university, and her excellent work record, the company decided to sponsor her studies in the United States to earn a graduate degree in computer science. The company sponsors few employees, and they have never sponsored a woman before. The company is very proud of Keiko and intends to make her their first woman manager once she completes her graduate degree. Her parents do not understand why she wants to study in the United States; they feel she should stay in Japan to help take care of her elderly grandparents.

Because her command of academic English is not sufficient for graduate school, her company has agreed to pay for six to nine months of English study in the United States before she begins her graduate program. She has been accepted into a graduate program at a large urban university on the condition that she obtain their required TOEFL® score by the spring semester. During the summer, Keiko enjoys living in the United States and studying at the university where she will do her graduate work. She progresses from an intermediate to an advanced ESL class because she is hardworking and diligent. Her teachers note the improvement in her oral skills and are surprised by her low TOEFL® score. She has taken the TOEFL® at every opportunity, but her scores remain far below the requirement for admission to graduate school.

After three months of study, and near the beginning of the fall semester, Keiko becomes seriously ill, has to drop out of school, and returns to Japan for medical treatment. After a month she returns but does not seem completely recovered; she is easily distracted and has trouble concentrating in class. One of her teachers, Ms. Madriz, asks Keiko to speak to her after class because she is concerned about her. Keiko confides to Ms. Madriz, and later to the director of the program, Mr. Amberton, that she cannot sleep, has no appetite, and has developed a recurring skin rash on her face. She is worried about passing the TOEFL® at the end of the semester. Keiko reports that her parents are worried about her, about her status in the company, and her future work opportunities if she cannot complete her degree as planned. Keiko points out that she is old and has obligations to the company and her parents to complete the graduate program as scheduled. Ms. Madriz and Mr. Amberton both suggest that she speak to a counselor as well as continue to receive medical attention. They fear that many of her medical problems are stress-related.

Despite the support and understanding of her teachers and Mr. Amberton, Keiko's health does not improve and her TOEFL® score improves only slightly by the end of the semester. Worried about her future, Keiko asks Ms. Madriz and Mr. Amberton to speak to the graduate admissions director and recommend that she be allowed to begin her graduate studies in the spring semester even if she does not have the required TOEFL® score. She argues that she is bright, works hard, and will do well in the graduate program. The TOEFL® is her only problem.

Questions for Discussion

1. What additional information would help you better understand this case?

2. What do you think are the causes of Keiko's stress? List them.

3. How do you think Ms. Madriz and Mr. Amberton feel about Keiko's situation?

4. What are arguments for Ms. Madriz and Mr. Amberton recommending that Keiko be admitted to the graduate program without the required TOEFL® score? What are the arguments against this option?

5. What could Ms. Madriz do if she and Mr. Amberton do not agree on what to recommend for Keiko in this case?

6. What are the options for Ms. Madriz? Mr. Amberton? Evaluate each option.

Extending the Case

Consider the three situations presented. Then reflect on these questions: (1) How does each situation differ from or relate to this case? (2) What contributing factors come into play in each situation? and (3) What are the possible courses of action for each?

1. A Cambodian student who is doing very well in her classes tells her grammar teacher that she gets so nervous during tests that she cannot concentrate or do her best. Her main problem is that she does not have enough time. She is worried about the upcoming final exam in the grammar class and asks to have extra time to complete the test.

2. A long-time instructor designs her reading and vocabulary course around the type of questions and material found on the new TOEFL® iBT (Internet-based test). She stresses that students need to practice test-taking skills and know what to expect on the standardized test. Some of her colleagues think that she is teaching to the TOEFL® iBT, but she counters that the test is important and that without a good score students will not be admitted. She also argues that teaching to the test will help them with their academic work once they are admitted.

3. A hardworking young woman from Guatemala needs a good score on a standardized English exam to be admitted to the Licensed Vocational Nurse (LVN) program at the community college. She has been studying in the adult school at night for two years while working to help her family with living expenses. She is a bright student. Despite this, she does poorly on exams and academic assignments. The day of the exam, she arrives and begins the exam, but 15 minutes into the test she asks to be excused, saying that she feels ill and needs to go to the restroom. After ten minutes, she returns to the testing room but says that she cannot finish the exam as she has been throwing up and is still nauseous.

Questions for Further Reflection

1. How can faculty and administrators address student stress associated with high-stakes testing? In classes? In program orientation and materials?

2. In what situations would it be advisable for a faculty member to talk to the program supervisor about a student's mental or physical difficulties related to test-taking? Give some examples.

3. Under what circumstances would it be appropriate for a student to be excused from a program-wide final? From a class final? From a standardized test?

4. What are some examples of situations where an exception to admission requirements to an undergraduate degree program is warranted? To a graduate program? To a trade school?

5. How can faculty and programs help ensure that high-stakes testing is fair and accurately assesses students' abilities?

6. How can faculty help students have less test anxiety?

7. Often students from other countries are familiar with high-stakes tests and cram schools where they prepare for such exams. Some see their goal in studying English as simply "passing the standardized test" (e.g., the TOEFL® iBT). How can faculty help students see the importance of learning English in general, not simply "studying for the test"?

8. What are some arguments for and against offering test preparation courses?

9. What are some arguments for and against using standardized tests as admission criteria?

10. Define an *exit test*. What are the arguments for and against having program exit tests?

11. Define *gatekeeper* in academic contexts. What role should English programs and faculty have as gatekeepers? What role should standardized tests have as gatekeepers?

Delving Deeper

1. Using the Internet and other resources, research the admission criteria for international undergraduates or graduates for three or more post-secondary institutions. You may wish to choose institutions that you are familiar with. Which standardized tests, if any, are used for admission purposes? What other criteria are used? Provide a short description of each criterion, explaining any standardized tests and the required scores needed, as well as the other criteria (e.g., high school or undergraduate GPA, personal statement). Present your findings in a chart and compare your results with others.

2. Different majors may require different TOEFL® scores. Check at least three different majors in one institution. What minimum scores are required for each? If there are differences in required scores, speculate as to why. What are the arguments for and against requiring different scores for different majors? Write about your findings, arguments, and reasons.

3. Choose one of the following topics as it applies to post-secondary institutions: (a) high-stakes testing, or (b) gatekeeping. Find two articles and write a summary and critique of both. Include your own opinion and document your sources appropriately.

Resources

Bachman, L. F., & Palmer, A. (1996). *Language testing in practice: Designing and developing useful language tests.* New York: Oxford.

Brown, J. D. (1996). *Testing in language programs: A comprehensive guide to English language assessment.* Upper Saddle River, NJ: Prentice-Hall Regents.

Douglas, D. (2006). *English language testing in U.S. colleges and universities* (2nd ed.). Washington, DC: NAFSA.

Hamp-Lyons, L. (1998). Ethical test preparation practice: The case of the TOEFL®. *TESOL Quarterly, 32*, 329–337.

———. (1999). Comments on Liz Hamp-Lyons' "Ethical test preparation practice: The case of TOEFL": The author responds . . . *TESOL Quarterly, 33*, 270–274.

Kadison, R., & DiGeronimo, T. F. (2004). Pressure and competition: Academic, extracurricular, parental, racial, and cultural. In *College of the overwhelmed: The campus mental health crisis and what to do about it* (pp. 35–64). San Francisco: Jossey-Bass.

Stoynoff, S., & Chapelle, C. A. (2005). *ESOL tests and testing*. Alexandria, VA: TESOL.

Wadden, P., & Hilke, R. (1999). Comments on Liz Hamp-Lyons' "Ethical test preparation practice: The case of the TOEFL": Polemic gone astray: A corrective to recent criticism of TOEFL preparation. *TESOL Quarterly, 33*, 263–270.

Resolution to the Featured Case

Ms. Madriz and Mr. Amberton told Keiko of their support and hope for her success. They assured her that they would speak to the graduate admissions officer and tell him that she was hard working, diligent, and bright. They said, however, that they could not ask him to waive the TOEFL® requirement. They also suggested that she take a break to regain her health and to work with counselors and others to learn to manage her stress. Once her health was better, she could begin her English studies again. She followed their advice and was able to pass the TOEFL® and begin her studies the following fall semester.

MY THOUGHTS on the Resolution

Case 24

Parental Pressure and Influence

Mr. Tim Masterson has taught in the IEP at a large urban university for many years. The program is a pre-academic program, with most of the students intending to enroll in undergraduate and graduate programs in the United States. Mr. Masterson is an excellent and demanding instructor. He is especially strict about attendance and has a policy stating that if students miss more than 20 percent of the classes for any reason, they fail the class. This is in line with the program's policy regarding attendance; however, the program's policy allows individual faculty to determine if an absence is excused or not excused. Mr. Masterson counts all absences as unexcused.

Yousef Al-Hatwar from Kuwait is enrolled in Mr. Masterson's elective, Business English. He is a pleasant young man and does good work. He, however, sometimes misses class, arrives late, and turns in assignments late. Yousef seldom offers an excuse for his absences or late assignments, replying if pressed that he was busy with other obligations, had a cold, or simply overslept. Mr. Masterson speaks to him several times about his poor attendance and uneven performance and attention to the work of the class. Yousef always listens politely, seems to take the advice well, but after a few classes falls back into his old habits.

Youself hopes to begin his degree program the following semester, has the required TOEFL® score, and only needs a C or 2.0 average in his courses this semester to be admitted. At the end of the semester, Yousef has a B average on his work and has missed slightly over 20 percent of the classes. Mr. Masterson records an F for him in the Business English class and submits his grades to the office to record. The day after submitting his grades, Ms. Cerny, the director, asks to speak to Mr. Masterson in her office. During their conversation, Ms. Cerny urges Mr. Masterson to change Yousef's grade to a C or C–. She argues that Yousef has done satisfactorily on the assigned work, has B or higher in all his other courses, and is capable of handling college courses. She then adds that Mr. Al-Hatwar, Yousef's father, is a big donor to the university.

Questions for Discussion

1. What additional information would help you better understand this case?

2. How do you think Yousef feels about studying in the program and in Mr. Masterson's class? About his grade in the class?

3. How do you think Mr. Masterson feels about Yousef's performance and behavior in his class?

4. What are some possible explanations for Ms. Cerny's request?

5. How do you think Ms. Cerny feels about requesting that Mr. Masterson change Yousef's grade?

6. How do you think Mr. Masterson feels about Ms. Cerny's request?

7. What are the implications of the power differential between Mr. Masterson and Ms. Cerny in this case?

8. What are some of the cultural and/or economic issues in this case, particularly as they relate to parental influence and expectations?

9. What options does Mr. Masterson have in this situation? Evaluate each option.

Extending the Case

Consider the three situations presented. Then reflect on these questions: (1) How does each situation differ from or relate to this case? (2) What contributing factors come into play in each situation? and (3) What are the possible courses of action for each?

1. A young Indonesian man speaks to his advanced grammar teacher after class about his academic plans for the next semester at the university. This semester he is studying in the IEP, but he has the required TOEFL® score and is accepted as an undergraduate in business for the following semester. As he is the oldest and only son, his father intends for him to take over the family business in Indonesia upon completion of his degree in the United States. In their discussion, the young man states that he has no interest in studying business or in taking over the family business. He would like to study photography

and film. However, he feels obligated to major in business and work in his father's company after college. He is not sure if he should tell his parents about his interests or not. He asks for advice from his instructor.

2. A young Indian woman, who has been studying at the language school for almost a year, is visibly upset in her conversation class one afternoon. After class, the instructor asks her if she is okay and if he can help her. She begins to cry and tells him that her parents want her to return home and marry the son of a family friend. She says that she does not love this man and, in fact, wants to marry her boyfriend, who is from Nebraska. He has proposed to her and has taken her to meet his parents, who approve of their planned marriage. She has not told her parents about her U.S. boyfriend and is unsure about what to do.

3. A student from Hong Kong asks his ESL writing instructor to allow him to advance to the freshman composition course the next semester at the community college. He is a hard-working student and does well in his classes, but the instructor believes he needs another semester of ESL writing instruction before he enrolls in freshman composition. The student goes on to explain the pressure that he is under to finish quickly and return to Hong Kong to work in the family business. His father has given him only four years to complete his degree, and if he has to take more English courses, he will not be able to complete his degree on schedule. In fact, he has not told his parents that he is taking any ESL courses. He fears what his father will say if he learns of his situation.

Questions for Further Reflection

1. What role should a director or administrator typically play in determining individual student course grades? In the application process?

2. What consideration in determining grades should be given to parents' or friends' contributions to the program or institution? To the prestige or standing of the student's parents or their connections (e.g., politicians, an upper administrator in the institution)?

3. List parental pressures that students may feel. Do these pressures cut across countries and cultures? Are some pressures more common in certain cultures than others? Explain your answers.

4. Which pressures seem prominent to you and your friends?

5. When students feel parental pressure, what role, if any, can faculty play in assisting and counseling students? Mediating for students?

6. What factors typically impact students' feelings about fulfilling family obligations? Do factors vary from culture to culture? Country to country? Family to family? Explain your answers.

7. What information can faculty or supervisors give to parents who request their child's grades, attendance, or general performance in classes?

Delving Deeper

1. Drawing on your educational experiences, think of two instances where your parent(s) or guardian(s) participated in your education in a positive way (e.g., assisting with a college application, talking to your teacher or principal on your behalf). Think of two instances where you feel that they may have intervened in a negative way (e.g., talking to your teacher or principal without your consent, urging you to major in a particular subject in college). Write about all four incidents and how you felt in each situation. Analyze and explain your reactions.

2. Share your description with a person from another country. Discuss your four incidents and find out how this individual would interpret your parents' behaviors and actions from his or her cultural perspective.

Resources

Coffey, M., & Grace, S. (1997). *Intercultural advising in English-language programs*. Washington, DC: NAFSA.

Family Educational Rights and Privacy Act (FERPA). www.ed.gov/policy/gen/guid/fpco/ferpa/index.html.

Kadison, R., & DiGeronimo, T. F. (2004). What parents can do. In *College of the overwhelmed: The campus mental health crisis and what to do about it* (pp. 183–212). San Francisco: Jossey-Bass.

Resolution to the Featured Case

At first Mr. Masterson was annoyed that Ms. Cerny asked him to consider changing Yousef's grade. He reviewed Yousef's work, grades, and attendance record. He also spoke to Yousef's other teachers, who admitted that they had given him the benefit of the doubt because he was a good language learner and bright. After careful thought, Mr. Masterson told Ms. Cerny that he would not change the grade because Yousef had too many absences. He admitted that he felt Yousef was capable of doing well as a university student. He suggested that Ms. Cerny inform Yousef of the grade appeal process should Yousef want to appeal his grade.

Ms. Cerny informed Yousef of the grade appeal process, but he did not appeal his grade. The university admitted Yousef as a regular undergraduate for the next semester, even though he had less than a 2.0 grade point average (GPA) (less than a C) in his IEP courses.

MY THOUGHTS **on the Resolution**

Case 25
Requests for Academic Assistance

Ms. McDonnell enjoys teaching her writing/speaking seminar for newly arrived international graduate students. Generally, she has students from a variety of academic fields: computer science, business, sports management, economics, environmental science, and education. The graduate students typically take two classes in their disciplines as well as the graduate writing/speaking seminar. The goals of Ms. McDonnell's class are to help students acculturate to graduate school in the university and to help them polish their English skills so that they can compete with native speakers in their classes. Wanting the class to be relevant to students' individual studies, Ms. McDonnell has students choose topics for their papers and speeches from their own disciplines. In addition, she asks students about the type of assignments that they are asked to do in their major classes and even spends class time helping students brainstorm about how to tackle assignments in their other classes.

Sometimes students ask Ms. McDonnell to help them outside of class with their papers for other classes, and she is glad to do this. A student who often asks for her assistance is Dmitri Schelyshev from Siberia. Almost every Tuesday afternoon, immediately after the graduate ESL class, he asks Ms. McDonnell to look over his economics paper that is due that evening. Ms. McDonnell does not like to refuse, so she helps him, even if it means she is late to a meeting. She starts to feel annoyed at Dmitri because the pattern persists even though she has reminded him several times that she has office hours Monday, Wednesday, and Friday mornings. Dmitri never comes to her office hours or arranges for an appointment at another time. He simply asks her for help at the end of class on Tuesdays. In fact, the situation is sometimes even worse. He sometimes arrives late to class on Tuesdays or fails to complete his work for Ms. McDonnell's class, yet still asks for her help with his economics papers.

Questions for Discussion

1. What additional information would help you better understand this case?

2. Why do you think Ms. McDonnell feels frustrated by this situation?

3. How does the basic structure of Ms. McDonnell's class possibly encourage Dmitri to take unfair advantage of Ms. McDonnell?

4. How do you think Ms. McDonnell viewed the situation with Dmitri at the beginning of the semester? How do you think her view has changed over the course of the semester?

5. What are some likely reasons for Dmitri's actions? How do you think he feels about asking Ms. McDonnell for help after class?

6. What responsibility does Ms. McDonnell have to help Dmitri with his economics papers?

7. Over the long term, what impact, if any, might Ms. McDonnell's helping Dmitri with his papers for other courses have on Dmitri and his English abilities?

8. How do you think Ms. McDonnell could minimize the possibility of such a situation developing in the future?

9. What different cultural norms, if any, does this case illustrate?

10. What options does Ms. McDonnell have at this point for dealing with the situation with Dmitri? Evaluate each option.

Extending the Case

Consider the three situations presented. Then reflect on these questions: (1) How does each situation differ from or relate to this case? (2) What contributing factors come into play in each situation? and (3) What are the possible courses of action for each?

1. An MBA faculty member tells one of his international students from Japan that he will not be able to pass his course if the student does not get help with his writing. The instructor informs the student that his papers have too many grammatical errors and are unacceptable. The student is distraught and unsure about what to do. He has worked long hours on each paper with assistance from the Writing Center on campus. He makes an appointment with the IEP director and asks her for a volunteer tutor, explaining that he is on a scholarship and has no extra money.

2. An individual from the People's Republic of China, who has no connection with the institution, meets with the director of a university IEP. During the meeting, the individual explains that she lives in the area and is applying as an undergraduate to several universities in other states. She would like help with her application, especially with the essays because her English writing skills are weak. When the director says that she can recommend some individuals and gives her the approximate cost per hour, the young woman interrupts and says that she has no money to pay for a tutor. She asks if the director or a teacher can simply help her for free.

3. Finals week is a busy time for students and instructors alike. One morning, an instructor receives a phone call from a former Mexican student asking him for an appointment to help with a research paper for his theology class. The student explains that there are no available appointments in the Writing Center, that he needs to do well on the paper or he will fail the class, and that the paper is due the next day at 9:00 AM.

Questions for Further Reflection

1. As a faculty member, what are arguments for and against assisting a student with written work for other classes?

2. What kind of assistance seems most appropriate for a faculty member to offer or agree to give in each of the following cases?

   a. a student currently enrolled in an instructor's class asking for help with papers for another class

   b. a former student asking for help with coursework

   c. a stranger from the community asking for free one-time editing of a resume

   d. a student the instructor does not know asking for free one-time assistance with a research paper

   e. an individual who is sent to a faculty member by his or her supervisor for limited assistance with one paper

   f. a student sent to a faculty member by another faculty member for assistance with ongoing coursework

3. How much help should a faculty member give a student with his or her paper for another class (e.g., a quick read and oral comments, correcting all the grammar errors, helping with organization, editing)? What do you think is an appropriate balance?

4. How can a faculty member determine the line between doing a paper for the student and the student doing the paper?

5. What responsibility, if any, does a student have to inform an instructor that he or she has received help with a paper? Does the responsibility differ depending upon the amount of help given the student?

6. What responsibility, if any, does a faculty member have to inform the student's instructor that he or she has helped the student? Does the responsibility differ depending upon the amount of help given the student?

7. What advice would you give a colleague who has trouble telling students who request assistance that he or she can only give them a limited amount of time or cannot help them at all?

8. What are examples of ways that faculty can be helpful to students, yet set limits and not feel taken advantage of?

9. List some reasons that faculty members feel stressed and experience burnout. Think of your own and your colleagues' experiences.

Delving Deeper

1. Faculty burnout is a common problem. From the Internet and other sources, develop definitions of the terms *burnout* and *work-life balance*. In a short essay, define these terms and explain how they relate to each other. Be prepared to share your work with others. Document your sources appropriately.

2. Using the Internet and other sources, develop a list of five to ten strategies that would help you personally either avoid burnout or achieve a good work-life balance. Exchange lists with two other people and discuss your lists. Find at least one more strategy from others' lists to add to yours. Try to implement the strategies on your list and keep the list as a reminder.

Resources

Bateson, M. C. (1989). *Composing a life*. New York: Penguin.

Casanave, C. P., & Sosa, M. (2007). *Respite for teachers: Reflection and renewal in the teaching life*. Ann Arbor: University of Michigan Press.

Clarke, M. A. (2003). *A place to stand: Essays for educators in troubled times*. Ann Arbor: University of Michigan Press.

———. (2007). *Common ground, contested territory: Examining the roles of English language teachers in troubled times*. Ann Arbor: University of Michigan Press.

Palmer, P. J. (1998). *The courage to teach: Exploring the inner landscape of a teacher's life*. San Francisco: Jossey-Bass.

Resolution to the Featured Case

Ms. McDonnell spoke to Dmitri, explaining that it was rude for him to arrive to class late, not submit his work on time, and then to ask for assistance with papers for his other classes. Dmitri apologized and became more conscientious about arriving to class on time. He frequently continued to turn in papers late and to ask for assistance with his other coursework. Ms. McDonnell decided that she would continue to help him and simply make sure not to get into a similar situation with students in the future.

Dmitri seemed appreciative of the help that Ms. McDonnell gave him with work for his graduate courses. After the semester had ended, he brought Ms. McDonnell a small box of chocolates and again said, "Thank you."

MY THOUGHTS on the Resolution

Case 26   Recommendations

Mr. Marchetti receives two emails from former students asking for letters of recommendation. Each has waived his right to see the letter and each request that the letter be sent within the next three weeks. The first student, Duong Hoang from Vietnam, is applying to graduate school in computer science at a prestigious U.S. university. Mr. Marchetti remembers Duong well from his advanced academic speaking class. Duong was a mature, hardworking student and one of the brightest students in the class. His speeches were always well organized and carefully planned. Duong's main problem is his pronunciation and his difficulty in communicating orally with others. Mr. Marchetti recalls that Duong is presently enrolled in a pronunciation class and thinks that perhaps his English has continued to improve.

Knut Solberg, a young man from Sweden, asks for a letter of recommendation for an undergraduate program in marketing. Mr. Marchetti remembers Knut as a likeable student whose English skills seemed to improve during the semester as much or more from activities outside of class as his work in class. He was an average student, earning a C in Mr. Marchetti's integrated skills class. Knut sometimes missed class, and he often submitted homework that was incomplete or late. Mr. Marchetti wonders if Knut's study skills have improved and if he is more serious about his studies now.

Mr. Marchetti decides to think about how to reply to each student before e-mailing each one.

Questions for Discussion

1. What additional information would help you better understand this case?

2. Why to do you think Duong and Knut each ask Mr. Marchetti and not another instructor for a recommendation?

3. What factors could make it difficult for Mr. Marchetti to come to a decision about writing in support of each of these students?

127

4. What kinds of replies can Mr. Marchetti give each student?

5. What additional information might help Mr. Marchetti make his decision about whether to write a letter for each of these students? Would you advise Mr. Marchetti to ask for additional information from Duong and Knut?

6. Assuming that Mr. Marchetti receives no additional information about each student and he agrees to write a letter for each, what information seems appropriate to include in each letter?

7. What information should Mr. Marchetti give to each student about the type of letter he intends to write?

8. If Mr. Marchetti decides not to write a letter, how should he explain his decision to each student?

9. What options does Mr. Marchetti have in each of these situations? Evaluate each option.

Extending the Case

Consider the three situations presented. Then reflect on these questions: (1) How does each situation differ from or relate to this case? (2) What contributing factors come into play in each situation? and (3) What are the possible courses of action for each?

1. A student from Somalia hears about an opening for a custodial position at the local public school in the rural community where he lives. He has a Green Card and is looking for work to help support his family. He knows that his adult education evening instructor, who has a daughter in the public school, is very involved with the school. He decides to ask his instructor for assistance in getting a custodial job at the public school. He requests that she put in a good word for him with the hiring committee.

2. An instructor at a community college receives a phone call from the director of the recreational center on campus. A student from Nicaragua has applied for a job working at the front desk of the recreational center. He gave the instructor's name as a reference. The instructor is surprised because the student never mentioned this to her. She likes the student personally and is confident that he would be helpful to

patrons of the center because he is friendly and personable. Additionally, she knows that he needs work to help support his family and to be able to continue his education. However, she feels that the student is not always responsible in that he often misses class and tends to do careless work. She is not sure what she should say.

3. At the end of the semester, a Swiss student asks her Business English instructor to write her a letter of recommendation for the university's MBA program. The instructor is unsure what to say. The student has scored well on the TOEFL® and on the GMAT®, and she has average grades in her undergraduate studies. She earned a C in the Business English class. However, the student generally isolated herself from others, and sometimes was on the verge of tears during class. Additionally, the student has confided to the instructor that she is depressed, has attempted suicide several times, and has been hospitalized for depression. At present, she is doing well, taking medication, and feels that she can be successful. Because of her psychological problems, she did not perform consistently in the Business English class, sometimes failing to submit assignments or submitting incomplete and unacceptable work. When her health was stable, however, she did good work. In addition to asking for a letter of recommendation, she asks her instructor for advice on how much information, if any, she should give about her depression in her personal statement as part of her application.

Questions for Further Reflection

1. Does the fact that a student waives or does not waive the right to see a letter of recommendation influence the contents of the letter? If so, how?

2. Is it always advisable to comment on a student's English language proficiency in a letter of recommendation? If not, when might it not be advisable?

3. In writing a letter of recommendation for a student, what are some examples of appropriate wording to accurately convey the student's functional level of English? List several examples.

4. To what extent are comments about a student's English proficiency a red flag in a letter of recommendation?

5. How much personal information about a student is appropriate for an instructor to comment on in a letter of recommendation?

6. What information can an instructor legally comment on in a letter of recommendation or when serving as a reference (e.g., personal factors such as socioeconomic situation, immigration status, marital status, physical and mental issues, health issues, disabilities)? To answer this question, you will need to do research on the Internet or elsewhere.

7. What is a reasonable amount of lead time to give an instructor when requesting a letter of recommendation (e.g., two days before the deadline, a week ahead of time)?

8. Under what conditions does it seem appropriate for an instructor to refuse to write a letter of recommendation?

9. How much information should an instructor give a student when refusing to write a letter of recommendation?

10. What kind of information is appropriate for an instructor to give a student when agreeing to write a letter of recommendation?

11. What factors should an ESL instructor consider when serving as a reference for a student who is applying for a job that does not require academic linguistic skills (e.g., custodian, front desk clerk, computer technician)?

12. What actions seem appropriate for an instructor to do to help students secure jobs on and off campus? What actions seem inappropriate in such situations?

13. Who, if anyone, should receive a copy of a student letter of recommendation (e.g., Dean's office, department head)?

Delving Deeper

Faculty members are often asked to write letters of recommendation for students. Doing so, however, can be time-consuming and difficult. Throughout the process, faculty members must make numerous decisions, the first one being whether or not to agree to write the letter.

1. Research the topic of writing letters of recommendation on the Internet and in print resources. Find guidelines for writing letters of recommendation and information about the types of information appropriate to include in such letters. You may also wish to look at sample letters. Find out the kinds of information an instructor can and cannot legally comment on in a letter or when serving as a reference (e.g., personal factors such as socioeconomic situation, immigration status, marital status, physical and mental health issues). Even if information about personal factors is legal, how much information is appropriate for an instructor to comment on? Write about your findings and be ready to share them with others. Document your sources appropriately.

2. Students from other countries may be unfamiliar with the concept of letters of recommendation. Using this concept as a teaching point, create a lesson about letters of recommendation. You may wish to draw up guidelines and a list of advice for students who need to request a letter of recommendation, including information about the process (e.g., how to decide whom to ask, when to ask, how to ask). Think about your own experience of asking for letters of recommendation. Use the Internet as well as print sources to find information. Share your lesson plan with others and document your sources appropriately.

3. Pretend that you are Mr. Marchetti and write a letter of recommendation for each of the students in the featured case: Duong Hoang and Knut Solberg.

Resources

Craig, D. (2005). *Letters of recommendation: All the hints, tips, and tricks you'll ever need to write lively letters that make a difference* (2nd ed.). Washington, MO: Paperbacks for Educators.

Whalley, S. (2000). *How to write powerful letters of recommendation*. Minneapolis, MN: Education Media.

Resolution to the Featured Case

Mr. Marchetti agreed to write letters for both Duong and Knut. He was honest in his assessment of each of them, indicating how well each had done in his class. In the letter for Duong, he praised Duong highly but did note that his pronunciation made it a challenge to understand him at times. He added that Duong was aware of this weakness and was diligently trying to improve his comprehensibility and clarity by taking classes and working with a private tutor. In the letter for Knut, he emphasized his good points and made no comment about his relaxed attitude.

Each student was accepted to the program to which he applied.

MY THOUGHTS **on the Resolution**

Case 27 Sponsored Events

As part of its summer English language travel and study program, a large West Coast university includes an overnight trip to a national park. The university subcontracts the excursion to a reputable tour company with a great deal of experience with international students. The tour company provides a guide, but the director of the program, Mrs. Colt, or another faculty member, always accompanies the group.

One summer, after a motor tour of the park in the afternoon, the bus arrives at a predetermined motel frequently patronized by the tour company, and students are assigned to their rooms. The following morning, the tour guide informs Mrs. Colt that another motel guest registered a complaint with the management of the motel about three Japanese students in her group. The guest told the management that the students in the adjacent room were very loud and apparently had partied until three o'clock in the morning. In addition, they smoked outside their room quite a bit, and the smoke had entered the other guests' room. According to the tour guide, the guests who lodged the complaint angrily demanded their money back, or a reduced charge, from the motel management.

Questions for Discussion

1. What additional information would help you better understand this case?

2. What kinds of information about behavior and etiquette would have been helpful to these students before going on the excursion?

3. To what extent can the students' alleged behavior in this situation be explained in terms of cultural differences? To what extent could the students' reported behavior be viewed as rude?

4. How could Mrs. Colt determine if the allegations are accurate?

5. If the allegations are true, what consequences to students, if any, might be appropriate in this case?

6. Assuming the complaints are valid, what could Mrs. Colt say to the hotel manager about the incident? What could she say if the complaints are not valid?

7. What options does Mrs. Colt have in handling this situation? What are the advantages and disadvantages of each option?

Extending the Case

Consider the three situations presented. Then reflect on these questions: (1) How does each situation differ from or relate to this case? (2) What contributing factors come into play in each situation? and (3) What are the possible courses of action for each?

1. During a class field trip to a local museum with a docent tour, a Finnish student receives a call on her cell phone and takes the call, speaking in her native language for several minutes. The student looks quite worried. The museum docent is obviously annoyed by this behavior.

2. An instructor incorporates a short service-learning segment into her course at an urban university. Students take public transportation to a local homeless shelter where they help prepare and serve a hot meal. Afterwards students write a journal entry about their experience. Most of the students write thoughtful and sensitive entries. A few write about "the dirty people" who came to the shelter and the "frightening and loud" young people on the bus. Some also write disturbing racist statements.

3. An instructor takes her high-intermediate class to a special exhibit on American foods at a local museum. She provides them with a worksheet with questions to answer about the exhibit. Once the students begin their museum visit, the instructor leaves.

Questions for Further Reflection

1. What are the benefits to students of sponsored events?

2. What are the benefits of service-learning experiences?

3. What are some ways an instructor can prepare students for these activities? List some specific issues relating to expected behaviors that would be appropriate to cover before any of these excursions.

4. What other responsibilities does an instructor have with respect to students' actions and behaviors during a sponsored event?

5. How may past participation in extracurricular activities in one's home country influence a student's reactions and behaviors on educational field trips in the U.S?

6. What types of sponsored activities seem appropriate for students at the college/university level? At the community college level? At the adult level?

7. List the strong points and the potential problems for each of the activities described in the featured case and the extensions.

8. What are some ways an instructor can handle negative reactions from students to service-learning or sponsored events?

9. What types of follow-up activities, if any, seem appropriate after students participate in sponsored events?

Delving Deeper

1. Identify three possible sponsored-event sites in your community. Identify the level of students (e.g., university, IEP, community college, or adult school). For each site, make a list with three columns. First, identify the benefits of the site. Next, identify the possible difficulties the site presents. Finally, briefly describe how you would handle each of these potential problems.

2. Develop a definition of service learning. You may wish to visit a service-learning center on campus or check the Internet for information. How does a service-learning component of a curriculum differ from a field trip? To what extent do you feel that a service-learning experience is or is not important for ESL students? Write a justification for your position.

Resources

Eyler, J., & Giles, D. (1999). *Where's the learning in service learning?* San Francisco: Jossey-Bass.

Eyring, J. L. (Ed.). (2006). Theme articles: Service-learning. *CATESOL Journal*, *18*(1), 21–95.

International Center for Service-Learning in Teacher Education. www.clemson.edu/icslte.

National Service-Learning Clearinghouse. www.servicelearning.org.

Resolution to the Featured Case

Mrs. Colt and the tour guide apologized to the hotel management for the behavior of the Japanese students. On the way home on the bus, the tour guide used the loudspeaker to explain to everyone what had happened and to talk about acceptable hotel/motel behavior. Mrs. Colt also told the students that they would discuss this issue again in their classes the following week.

MY THOUGHTS on the Resolution

Case 28 Students and the Legal System

One morning at 9:00 AM, Chutima, a 24-year-old affluent graduate student from Bangkok, hears a knock on her apartment door. She opens the door and is handcuffed by U.S. Immigration and Customs Enforcement (ICE) agents who discovered some irregularities in her I-20 paperwork. She is taken to jail immediately. Later in the day, she contacts her boyfriend who then contacts the international student advisor at the university where she is studying. Both drive to the jail, and her boyfriend pays the $15,000 bail. Chutima is thus able to return to her apartment, but the authorities keep both her passport and her state identification card. A date for a hearing is set, and Chutima hires a lawyer.

Chutima had been accepted at and granted I-20s from two universities in the same city. One university, therefore, reported to immigration officials that she never enrolled in their institution. Thus, federal agents started looking for her and were easily able to locate her. When she was arrested, Chutima maintained that she turned in the correct paperwork to the second university she was attending and that it was their responsibility to see that the appropriate documents and information were recorded with ICE.

Chutima is traumatized. She informs Dr. Hurtado, her instructor and advisor, about the details of her ordeal by email but never makes an appointment to meet. She is so distraught and humiliated by the experience that she stops coming to class and asks for an extension for all of her papers that are due. She tells a friend that she is ashamed and embarrassed to come to class or see anyone she knows.

Questions for Discussion

1. What additional information would help you better understand this case?

2. How do you think Chutima feels in this situation? Why?

3. What is the institutional responsibility to a student in Chutima's situation?

4. How could Dr. Hurtado encourage Chutima to return to class?

5. How much latitude seems advisable for Dr. Hurtado to allow for late papers, missed work, and absences in this case?

6. To what extent does it seem appropriate for Dr. Hurtado to discuss a situation of this nature with the class, keeping in mind that other students might also encounter legal problems? Explain your opinion.

7. What explanation could there be for Chutima's behavior (e.g., her use of email and reluctance to attend class)? Do you think cultural issues play a role in her response?

8. What is the concept of saving face? What role do you think cultural differences play in the concept of saving face in an academic situation?

9. What are some ways cultural differences related to the concept of saving face could manifest themselves in class?

10. To what extent is the incident described a reflection of the climate in the United States since the events of September 11, 2001?

11. What options does Dr. Hurtado have in dealing with Chutima? What are the advantages and disadvantages of each?

Extending the Case

Consider the three situations presented. Then reflect on these questions: (1) How does each situation differ from or relate to this case? (2) What contributing factors come into play in each situation? and (3) What are the possible courses of action for each?

1. A student from Taiwan in a university IEP speaks to the director of the program and each of his teachers, telling them that he needs to return home because his grandmother is very ill. With the help of the director, the student obtains the necessary signatures; his instructors agree that his absences will be excused, and he will make up any missed work upon his return. Several weeks later he has not returned or replied to any emails from the program staff, so everyone assumes that he is still home helping his grandmother. A few weeks later, a classmate says that she has seen the student at a popular club. The director finally makes contact with the student. After almost six weeks, he comes into the program office and tells the director he only returned the day before.

The director checks with the international student advisor about the situation and learns that according to the student's SEVIS (Student Exchange and Visitor System Information System) record, the student returned to the U.S. three weeks ago.

2. A student from the Slovak Republic comes to his instructor during office hours. He explains that he got a ticket for making a right turn on red where a sign that said *No right turn on red* was posted. The sign was covered by a tree branch, and the student shows his instructor a photo he took at the scene, in which the tree clearly covers the sign. He intends to show this photo to the authorities. He excitedly asks his instructor whether or not he should go ahead with his plan of challenging the ticket. He also asks if she thinks he is going to win his case, if he could be excused from class for the hearing, how this will affect his status in the United States, and whether or not he will need to go to Washington, D.C. to straighten out this matter.

3. Upon entering the classroom before the evening class begins, the instructor notices a group of Hispanic women huddled together and talking rapidly and excitedly in Spanish. While it is common for students to chat before class, the pitch of conversation is much higher than usual. The instructor cautiously approaches the group and overhears their conversation about an immigration raid at two local restaurants the previous day. It seems that several of the students know individuals who were arrested for working illegally.

Questions for Further Reflection

1. To what extent does an instructor have a responsibility to assist a student with legal issues?

2. What are an institution's responsibilities to the U.S. legal system, specifically to the U.S. Department of Homeland Security and its internal divisions such as ICE and the United States Citizenship and Immigration Services (USCIS)?

3. Is it appropriate for an instructor to inquire about the immigration status of his or her students? Why or why not?

4. What are some ways an institution can deal with a student who deliberately defies U.S. laws and/or university regulations?

5. What are some ways an institution can assist students who inadvertently make an error or misunderstand the U.S. legal system and /or university regulations?

6. What kinds of reactions do you think students have when dealing with the U.S. legal system for the first time? Could these reactions be influenced by their experiences in their native countries? Explain your answer.

7. To what extent do students need to understand the laws at different levels of government in the United States? At the local level? At the state level? At the federal level?

8. What role does an instructor of a citizenship class have in helping students with the process of applying for citizenship and for doing well on the test?

Delving Deeper

1. Go to the U.S. Immigration and Customs Enforcement home page. Examine the information presented. Then enter ICE: SEVIS (Immigration and Customs Enforcement: Student Exchange and Visitor Information System) into your search engine. Compare the difference in tone in those two pages. Write about your reflections on these differences.

2. Evaluate the U.S. Citizenship and Immigration Services (USCIS) website. Write about your overall reaction, reflect on the tone and information, and describe how you think an immigrant or refugee might react to or interpret the website.

3. Interview an international or immigrant student about the step-by-step process of entering the United States. Write about your findings and be prepared to share them. From your perspective, was the process onerous? Was it acceptable? What, if anything, about the process might have been improved?

Resources

Goffman, E. (1959). *The presentation of self in everyday life*. Garden City, NY: Doubleday.

NAFSA: Association of International Educators. www.nafsa.org.

Nguyen, T. (2005). *We are all suspects now: Untold stories from immigrant America after 9/11*. Boston: Beacon Press.

TESOL: Teachers of English to Speakers of Other Languages. www.tesol.org.

U.S. Citizenship and Immigration Services (USCIS). www.immigrationdirect. com/indexv1.htm.

U.S. Committee for Refugees and Immigrants. www.refugees.org.

U.S. Immigration and Customs Enforcement. www.ice.gov.

Resolution to the Featured Case

Unfortunately, Dr. Hurtado was never officially informed about exactly what had happened to Chutima. Her main sources of information were the other students, the local newspapers, and Chutima's email correspondence. From the newspaper, Dr. Hurtado learned that all charges against Chutima were eventually dropped. She allowed Chutima to complete all classwork outside of class, including the final exam. Chutima returned to Bangkok immediately at the end of the semester. She never finished the program.

MY THOUGHTS on the Resolution

Case 29

Dangerous and Uncomfortable Situations

Paivi Konti, a Fulbright exchange scholar from Finland, and her Finnish friend, Ulla, have a graduate computer science class together at a large urban campus on the East Coast. It ends at 7:00 in the evening. After class, they generally go out for supper together at a nearby fast food restaurant and then walk back to the graduate dorm, taking a shortcut along the edge of the campus. By the time they finish their supper, it is dark. One evening they sense that someone is following them. It is not just one person, but two. The two strangers catch up to the women, stop them, and demand their laptops at knifepoint. The students hand over their laptops and the thieves run away. The women stand for a moment, dumbfounded. Paivi does all of her banking online and wonders how secure these systems really are. Ulla wonders when she last backed up her paper for her economics class. The two women do not know what to do next and are terrified.

Questions for Discussion

1. What additional information would help you better understand this case?

2. To what extent did the two women act in the most sensible way to reduce their risk of physical harm?

3. How can an academic institution assist students in avoiding a situation such as this one?

4. How can an academic institution assist students after an incident such as this one?

5. What knowledge about the U.S. legal system would be helpful to the women in this situation?

6. What lessons can be learned about the importance of backing up one's computer files? About keeping financial information secure?

7. What would you suggest Paivi do? Ulla?

Extending the Case

Consider the three situations presented. Then reflect on these questions: (1) How does each situation differ from or relate to this case? (2) What contributing factors come into play in each situation? and (3) What are the possible courses of action for each?

1. A student from Japan wants to have American friends so that he can really practice his English and learn more about American culture. He makes several acquaintances, and one evening they invite him to go along to a local bar to have a couple of beers and play some pool. Late in the evening, his American friends offer him a joint of marijuana. He has never used drugs before and does not intend to now. He is not sure how to refuse and how to leave.

2. A young woman from El Salvador takes the bus to and from her English class two evenings a week after work. One night, on her way home, a drunk man gets on the bus and sits next to her even though there are only a few people on the bus and many other available seats. She wants to move, but because she is sitting by the window, it is difficult for her to do so.

3. A shy Asian woman patiently waits until everyone except her instructor has left the classroom. She then asks her instructor to help her with a personal problem. She says that she received an anonymous call from a man who told her that she had won a new warm-up suit. He asked her what size she wears and commented on how sexy she would look in this new outfit. He stated that he would call again with more information about how to collect her prize.

Questions for Further Reflection

1. List four or five safety issues and concerns for students in the United States. Which of these could be of concern to your students? Which of these might not be an issue or concern in other countries?

2. What are some essential safety issues an instructor should introduce to all students?

3. What information related to computer and Internet security is appropriate for faculty to incorporate into their curricula (e.g., information related to PIN numbers, posting online, backing up files, social networking)?

4. What are some ways instructors can incorporate information about personal safety into the curriculum?

5. What specific English phrases can students learn to better cope with people with whom they prefer not to interact?

6. How can instructors effectively present safety information without scaring students?

7. How can academic institutions assist students with safety issues?

8. What local services are available to faculty and students to assist them in learning and practicing behaviors that will help to keep them safe?

9. What are some of the stereotypes international and immigrant students have about crime in the United States? Which do you think are well-founded? Which are simply stereotypes?

Delving Deeper

1. Develop an introductory lesson about a safety issue in your community. These issues will differ from community to community. For example, on the West Coast, the issue might be earthquake safety. In another area, it could be street crime. List important vocabulary related to the issue and the classroom exercises and activities you would use. Have necessary emergency phone numbers available for students. Identify the type of program and the level of your students (e.g., adult night school, intermediate).

2. Plan a special class or assembly with a campus public safety or local police officer. In your planning, determine the types of issues that you feel need to be covered (access to emergency numbers, how to talk to a police officer, etc.). Make an outline of your ideas to share with others.

Resources

Hafernik, J. J., Vandrick, S., & Messerschmitt, D. S. (2000). Safety issues for international students in the United States. *TESL Reporter*, *33*(2), 1–9.

Help Guide. www.helpguide.org.

Leki, R. S. (2008). *Travel wise: How to be safe, savvy and secure abroad*. Boston: Intercultural Press.

National Center for Victims of Crimes. www.ncvc.org/ncvc.Main.aspx.

Wilkinson, C. K., & Rund, J. A. (Eds.). (2002). *Addressing contemporary campus safety issues: New directions for student services* (no. 99). San Francisco: Jossey-Bass.

Resolution to the Featured Case

Paivi and Ulla reported the theft to campus public safety personnel who then called the police. The campus public safety personnel told them exactly what steps to follow to make sure there would not be a problem with identity theft. Ulla had not backed up her work and had to reconstruct her paper on a laptop borrowed from a friend. Both women needed to buy new laptops and used the campus escort service to return home directly after class for the remainder of the semester.

MY THOUGHTS on the Resolution

Case 30 Possible Abusive Situations

Mrs. Annie Tam from Hong Kong is a woman in her thirties who is trying to improve her English at the local night school. She seems very serious and extremely earnest. She also seems to be constantly on edge and always sits close to the door. Because the class runs from 7:00–10:00 PM on Tuesday and Thursday evenings, the instructor, Mrs. Noble, gives the students a ten-minute break at about 8:30. Most of the students get coffee and beverages at the vending machines and chat with each other. Mrs. Tam, however, leaves the class first, seemingly in a hurry, and runs outside. She is always the last to return, sometimes after the class has resumed, and quietly takes her seat near the door. Toward the end of class, she begins to pack up her papers, and then, at the end of class, she again leaves very quickly. At the middle of the semester, after she has gotten more acquainted with her students, Mrs. Noble casually comments to Mrs. Tam that she always seems in a hurry. Mrs. Tam replies that she has no time to talk as she needs to check on her two children, ages three and five, who are waiting in the car during class with their grandmother who does not speak any English.

Questions for Discussion

1. What additional information would help you better understand this case?

2. To what extent could the situation described in this case be considered acceptable? Could it be a case of neglect or endangerment?

3. At what point should this situation be reported to an administrator? To legal authorities? If this situation does not seem problematic, under what circumstances do you think it could become problematic (cold weather, for example)?

4. Are there ways Mrs. Noble could assist Mrs. Tam in this situation?

5. Re-examine Case 11 about classroom visitors. What major issue or issues are involved in both cases?

6. To what extent is this case an example of a situation that is borderline problematic?

Extending the Case

Consider the two situations presented. Then reflect on these questions: (1) How does each situation differ from or relate to this case? (2) What contributing factors come into play in each situation? and (3) What are the possible courses of action for each?

1. A woman from the Czech Republic, who lives with her partner, comes to class with a black eye. When asked by fellow students what happened, she says she fell down. Two weeks later, the same student appears with a large bruise on her arm. Again she says that she fell down.

2. In conversation class, a very talkative middle-aged Spanish-speaking woman always complains about her husband. She says that he tells her that her dinners are bad on the nights when she comes to class. She says he will not allow her to go out with the other students for coffee after class; he wants her to come home right away. He also says he does not like her hair and that she is not very smart.

Questions for Further Reflection

1. List the types of abusive situations students might encounter or find themselves in.

2. How do cultural differences affect students' views of what may or may not constitute an abusive situation? What role does the legal system in their native country play in these views?

3. What are the laws in your state regarding the reporting of child abuse? Of adult abuse?

4. What is the responsibility of an instructor to follow up on information on potentially unsafe or abusive situations that students either inadvertently or intentionally relate in class?

5. What are arguments for and against an instructor incorporating a presentation in class on recognizing and dealing with different types of abuse?

6. What kinds of campus and community resources are available to instructors who suspect abuse of any kind in their students' lives? What resources can instructors recommend to students who may be in abusive situations?

Delving Deeper

1. Research two websites for state or national agencies with local affiliates that deal with abusive situations. For example, you might choose a shelter for battered women and a center that helps individuals manage their anger. Write a description of the agencies, providing contact information and the types of services offered. Evaluate their outreach programs for people who don't speak English, and then develop new outreach services for each of the agencies to encourage individuals who do not speak English to avail themselves of the services offered.

2. Public health campaigns are common in many countries, with announcements and advertisements on radio, television, and on billboards. For example, there may be public health campaigns about domestic violence or about HIV/AIDS. These campaigns may touch on risky behaviors, abusive situations, physical and mental health issues, or safety issues. Spend time in your community observing radio, television, and public advertisements regarding these issues. Keep a log of the types of issues addressed, the medium of delivery, the location (i.e., if it is a billboard or sign), and any other interesting information. What conclusions can you draw (e.g., Which issues are given priority? Who is the targeted audience?). Write about your findings and conclusions to share with others. If you are familiar with other countries, share your impressions of their public health campaigns.

Resources

Burak, P. A., & Hoffa, W. W. (2001). *Crisis management in a cross-cultural setting* (Rev. ed.). Washington, DC: NAFSA.

Centers for Disease Control and Prevention (CDC) Health and Safety for College Students. www.cdc.gov/Features/collegehealth.

Helpguide. www.helpguide.org.

National Center for Victims of Crime (NCVC). www.ncvc.org.

Resolution to the Featured Case

Mrs. Noble spoke to the director of the program about the situation. The director checked the car outside and found the children with their grandmother playing games. It was a comfortable spring evening, and everyone was fine. Mrs. Noble asked Annie what she would do if the weather were cold. She said she did not know, and the situation continued.

MY THOUGHTS on the Resolution

Case 31   Selecting Materials

Mrs. Prador teaches in a large community college. She recently read an article (Liu, 2004) and a book, *Going Graphic* (Cary, 2004), on using comics and other graphics in teaching L2 reading, vocabulary, and conversation. She knows that comics are extremely popular in many countries, and she thinks that they might be effectively used in her classroom activities. She selects a Peanuts® strip by the late Charles Schultz and whites out the words in the bubbles. The assignment is for students to work in small groups and write their own language in the bubbles. She has repeated the assignment several times and finds that the students are highly engaged not only with the language itself but also with the cultural insights the strip provides. Pleased with her success, she presents her comic strip project to her colleagues at a faculty meeting. Ms. Charleston, a colleague, objects to her presentation, claiming that comic strips are not an appropriate introduction to English for non–English speaking students. She argues that even if Peanuts® is a relatively good example of comics, using the medium in class encourages the students to examine other comic strips that might contain improper English. Therefore, she does not approve of Mrs. Prador's use of comics as appropriate material and asks the curriculum coordinator to intervene.

Questions for Discussion

1. What additional information would help you better understand this case?

2. To what extent are comics appropriate material for use in an ESL classroom? Are some comics more appropriate than others?

3. Are some comics more appropriate for certain age or ethnic groups?

4. List several pedagogical arguments for using comic strips in class.

5. How could Mrs. Prador introduce activities to students to point out the advantages of their use?

6. What could Mrs. Prador do if the students had complained about the use of comics?

150

7. How familiar might students be with comic books and graphic novels?

8. How do you think Mrs. Prador feels about Ms. Charleston?

9. Why do you think Ms. Charleston disapproves so strongly of comics?

10. What options does the curriculum coordinator have in this situation? Evaluate each option.

Extending the Case

Consider the three situations presented. Then reflect on these questions: (1) How does each situation differ from or relate to this case? (2) What contributing factors come into play in each situation? and (3) What are the possible courses of action for each?

1. An instructor decides to do a vocabulary lesson on profanity in English since so many students have asked questions about profane terminology. She informs her students at the class meeting the day before the scheduled lesson and asks if anyone wants to be excused. After class, one student approaches the instructor and asks to be excused. The next day, after class, another student complains that she did not understand what the class was going to be about and she was very embarrassed by the content.

2. An instructor regularly brings in episodes from popular TV shows such as *The Simpsons* and *The Sopranos* for listening comprehension lessons. A student from Singapore asks if these tapes are examples of good English and complains about the violence on *The Sopranos*.

3. The instructor of the advanced reading course in an IEP complains to the director that the instructor teaching the high-intermediate reading class is using an inappropriate textbook, one that is too advanced. He asks the director if any of the students have complained that the book is too hard. The director says she is not aware of a problem. The instructor notes that the back cover of the text states that the book is appropriate for "high-intermediate/advanced" students. He indicates that he had planned to use this text next semester with his advanced class, but now he cannot. He insists that the director speak to the faculty member currently using the book and check all future book orders carefully to prevent such situations from occurring.

Questions for Further Reflection

1. How appropriate is it for one instructor to object to and try to prevent another instructor from using certain activities or materials? If you think it seems appropriate to intervene, suggest some ways for an instructor to do this respectfully.

2. What are some examples of materials and topics of discussion that might not be appropriate for ESL classes?

3. What is an instructor's obligation to take action if a colleague seems to be using material inappropriate for the students' level?

4. What are some ways a supervisor can address differences of opinion among faculty regarding appropriate learning materials?

5. To what extent and how should instructors deal with questionable course content (e.g., swear words)?

Delving Deeper

1. Many instructors like to use videos and DVDs in class, often developing a unit or theme around a single film. Evaluate a movie such as Will Smith's *Pursuit of Happyness* in terms of its appropriateness for classroom use. List the attributes of the film and why it might work. Consider issues such as content, theme, language, violence, and sex. Be prepared to share your list.

2. Develop a list of three or four of your favorite films. Which ones might be appropriate for classroom use? List the attributes of each film that you feel are appropriate for use in an ESL class. Think of a film you like that might not work in an ESL class. List the reasons why. Be prepared to share all of your selections.

3. Make a list of five to ten books, fiction and nonfiction, that seem appropriate for ESL students. Specify the context (e.g., intermediate level with 20- to 30-year-old students). Next to each book, give reasons for its appropriateness. Prepare to discuss your list and reasons with others.

Resources

Cary, S. (2004). *Going graphic*. Portsmouth, NH: Heinemann.

Liu, J. (2004). Effects of comic strips on L2 learners' reading comprehension. *TESOL Quarterly, 38* (2), 225–243.

Shulman, M. (2009). *Cultures in contrast: Student life at U.S. colleges and universities* (2nd ed.). Ann Arbor: University of Michigan Press.

Summerfield, E., & Lee, S. (2006). *Seeing the big picture: A cinematic approach to understanding cultures in America* (Rev. ed.). Ann Arbor: University of Michigan Press.

Resolution to the Featured Case

Both Mrs. Prador and the curriculum coordinator agreed that the use of comics in this case was appropriate and not a problem. However, the faculty later had a discussion about what types of material and subjects might not be appropriate.

MY THOUGHTS on the Resolution

Case 32 Faculty Personal Agendas

Mr. Miller teaches at the local community college where he has been on the faculty for 15 years. He began his career after a Peace Corps assignment in Peru. While in Peru, he developed two lifelong commitments: teaching ESL and preserving the environment. In Peru, he had witnessed a great deal of environmental damage. Thus, he belongs to three environmental protection groups and keeps up-to-date on environmental issues worldwide. Whenever possible, he uses environmental issues as prompts for writing assignments and springboards for discussion. Topics have included building the dam on the Yangtze River, clear-cutting in the American Northwest, water pollution in India, and the slaughtering of whales in Japan. At midterm, a group of five students asks Mr. Miller if they can speak to him after class. The spokesperson for the group politely tells Mr. Miller that they are tired of environmental issues and want to study something else. In addition, they feel that they are being coerced into criticizing their own countries, and they are reluctant to do that. Mr. Miller responds that there is nothing more important than the environment and that he will not change the assignments. The students later make an appointment with the department chair.

Questions for Discussion

1. What additional information would help you better understand this case?

2. Content-based instruction is an important part of second language instruction. What are some determining factors in selecting appropriate content for classroom use?

3. In this case, to what extent might the students be worried that by speaking to Mr. Miller their grades might be jeopardized?

4. To what extent do you think Mr. Miller responds appropriately to the students?

5. How can Mr. Miller best respond to the assertion that he coerces students to criticize their own governments?

154

6. To what extent do you see this case as an issue of academic freedom for both the instructor and the students in his class?

7. What options does Mr. Miller's department chair have in this case? Evaluate each option.

Extending the Case

Consider the three situations presented. Then reflect on these questions: (1) How does each situation differ from or relate to this case? (2) What contributing factors come into play in each situation? and (3) What are the possible courses of action for each?

1. In a recent election, the instructor's candidate of choice did not win. Dismayed at the outcome, the next day she felt that it was very important to discuss the implications of the election with her writing class and did so for about 30 minutes.

2. An instructor has two children, Harry and Dominic, ages five and seven respectively. The instructor learned a lot watching their first language development and feels that their experience could be related to the classes she teaches. In addition, she feels her children are extremely bright. Therefore, she talks about her children at least once in every class, using them as examples for her lessons. In teaching the comparative form of adjectives, for example, she says, "Harry is younger than Dominic."

3. When the Olympic torch passed through a large Western city on the way to the 2008 Olympics in Beijing, China, an IEP instructor went to the route and demonstrated with a large banner saying "Free Tibet now!" After the demonstration, she rushed back to her class with the banner and placed it in front of the room in full view of her students, three of whom were from the People's Republic of China.

Questions for Further Reflection

1. How much of one's personal interests, such as family and hobbies, is appropriate for an instructor to present and use as content in class? How much of one's political and religious views?

2. What is the difference between advocacy and coercion? Provide some examples of each. When does advocating a position cross the line and go beyond advocacy? Give an example.

3. To what extent should students make suggestions about curriculum content?

4. To what extent should an instructor implement student suggestions about the curriculum?

5. How does the power differential between the instructor and the students impact the classroom and faculty-student interactions regarding curriculum decisions?

6. When is it appropriate for students to go over the head of an instructor to the next level of administration?

Delving Deeper

1. Academic freedom is an important part of education today. It allows instructors to teach openly about some very controversial and often unpopular issues without fear of reprisal. Find at least two sources on the issue of academic freedom. What does the term mean? Why is it important? Develop and write a working definition of the term and explain how it relates to the issues raised in the featured case and Extension 1.

2. Using the Internet and other resources, define *content-based instruction*. What are the benefits and risks of using content-based instruction? What are two or three ways Mr. Miller could minimize the risk and keep the students interested and motivated? Write about your findings and prepare to discuss them with others.

Resources

American Association of University Professors (AAUP). www.aaup.org.

Hafernik, J. J., Messerschmitt, D. S., & Vandrick, S. (2002). Academic freedom. In *Ethical issues for ESL faculty: Social justice in practice* (pp. 128–133). Mahwah, NJ: Lawrence Erlbaum.

Lunsford, A. (1996). Afterthoughts on the role of advocacy in the classroom. In P. M. Sparks (Ed.), *Advocacy in the classroom: Problems and possibilities* (pp. 432–437). New York: St. Martins Press.

Pally, M. (Ed.). (1999). *Sustained content teaching in academic ESL/EFL: A practical approach.* Boston: Houghton Mifflin.

Snow, M.A., & Brinton, D. M. (Eds.). (1997) *The content-based classroom: Perspectives on integrating language and content.* White Plains, NY: Addison-Wesley/Longman.

Resolution to the Featured Case

Mr. Miller's department chair listened to the students and assured them he would speak to Mr. Miller. He also assured them that they had made the correct decision to come forward with the issue. In a meeting with Mr. Miller, the chair had several suggestions about other topics of interest that the class might welcome. Mr. Miller said he would try some of them. Evidently he did because the students did not complain a second time.

MY THOUGHTS on the Resolution

Case 33

Faculty Personal Issues

Mr. Harris has taught for 20 years in his local community college district where he has a full-time position with tenure. From time to time, he cancels class, saying he is sick.

Recently, over the course of the semester, the students in his writing class begin to suspect that he has an alcohol problem because he sometimes smells strange and has slurred speech. Most days his behavior seems fine in class, but occasionally his lessons are unfocused and his behavior erratic. The students become more and more certain of his problem as the semester progresses. They do not think he is a very good teacher, but at the same time, they are worried about him. After much discussion outside of class, they determine that Mrs. Tanaka, a Japanese student who is the oldest student in the class, should speak to Ms. Owens, a part-time instructor in the oral communication class, about Mr. Harris. Ms. Owens is a young and delightful instructor, whom the students all love. Mrs. Tanaka comes to Ms. Owens' desk one morning before class, identifies herself as the class spokesperson, and relates the suspicions of the group regarding Mr. Harris. Mrs. Tanaka asks her to help, but cautions her that the students in Mr. Harris' class do not want to be implicated in any way.

Questions for Discussion

1. What additional information would help you better understand this case?

2. Why do you think the class decided to talk to another instructor rather than to the program director?

3. What other problems might account for Mr. Harris' behavior?

4. If Mr. Harris' behavior is not related to alcoholism but rather medical in nature, how would that fact change this situation? How do you think a suspected medical situation should be handled?

5. What are some legal or privacy issues that could be involved in this case?

6. What are some possible courses of action for Ms. Owens in this case?

Extending the Case

Consider the three situations presented. Then reflect on these questions: (1) How does each situation differ from or relate to this case? (2) What contributing factors come into play in each situation? and (3) What are the possible courses of action for each party involved?

1. An instructor has been a faculty member at a local community college for thirty years. He currently teaches writing. At some point in his life, he developed a hearing loss in one ear and now has difficulty hearing and understanding his students, especially since they have a variety of different accents. He has notified students of his problem on the syllabus, but a student from Morocco complains to the administration, stating that Mr. Dobbs should not be teaching.

2. The program director notices on several occasions that an instructor in the Saturday morning adult class at the local high school arrives at the school 10–20 minutes after the class is scheduled to begin. The students have learned that he is always late, so they come to class later as well. He always dismisses class on time because several students need to catch the bus.

3. Recently a full-time instructor moved his family to his mother's house because she is no longer able to live alone. This move means that he and his wife now have a one-and-one-half-hour commute each way to work, and his children have changed schools. Because of his family obligations, the instructor can rarely attend faculty meetings or social events on campus for students. He comes to campus, teaches his classes, holds office hours, and returns home.

Questions for Further Reflection

1. List some common examples of personal problems faculty may have. If a colleague is aware of the problem, how might he or she help? An administrator?

2. How do cultural mores influence students' decisions about how to deal with a faculty member who has a personal issue?

3. What are some ways an instructor or director can handle student complaints about a colleague when the issue is clearly medical (e.g., arthritis or deafness)?

4. What are some ways an instructor or administrator can handle student complaints about a colleague's habits or behaviors, such as consistent tardiness?

5. To what extent, and in what ways, should an instructor or administrator attempt to verify complaints about a colleague?

6. Under what circumstances should an instructor take a student complaint to a higher level of authority? Under what circumstances should an instructor refer the students directly to a higher level of authority?

7. To what extent do power differentials among faculty, (e.g., tenured status, gender, age) influence an instructor's decision to deal with a colleague's personal problems?

8. To what extent does the type of faculty problem determine a course of action for a supervisor? What legal implications must be considered?

Delving Deeper

1. List some possible faculty issues that might be problematic in the classroom or in interaction with colleagues. For example, you might consider issues such as alcoholism, drug addiction, illness, hearing loss, and the like. Which might be accommodated and how? Which may be particularly difficult to address? You may wish to consult the ADA (Americans with Disabilities Act) website. Discuss your reasons with others.

2. If you are new to the field, interview an experienced faculty member about dealing with colleagues who have personal issues that affect work performance. If you are experienced, try to recall a situation in which you were concerned about a colleague's personal situation or well-being. In either instance, using assumed names, write a description of the incident or ongoing situation and describe what happened. Reflect on the extent to which the situation was successfully resolved or not.

Resources

Americans with Disabilities Act. www.ada.gov.

National Center on Addiction and Substance Abuse. www.casacolumbiz.org.

Resolution to the Featured Case

Based on her own observations, Ms. Owens suspected that Mr. Harris had a serious drinking problem. Therefore, she decided to talk to the director about him. She reported to Mrs. Tanaka that she had spoken to the director who promised to address the issue with Mr. Harris. Ms. Owens received no additional information about the matter. Mr. Harris' behavior did not change.

MY THOUGHTS **on the Resolution**

Case 34 Romance at School and Work

Kelly Rose, a popular and dedicated instructor at a community college, comes into the department chair's office one evening after class; she is visibly upset. She tells the chair, Mr. Albert Duncan, about news that she just received from a trustworthy student in her grammar class. According to Ms. Rose's source, Anna Mendoza, a 22-year-old immigrant from Nicaragua also in her grammar class, is romantically involved with the coordinator of the computer center, Mr. Sawyer. Mr. Sawyer, a long-time employee at the college, is in his forties, married, and has two teenage children. In talking about the alleged situation, Ms. Rose becomes more and more outraged, recounting that her student said that Mr. Sawyer has bought Anna expensive gifts and taken her on weekend trips. Mr. Duncan listens attentively and recalls that Anna works in the computer center three evenings a week and is often in the student lounge with Mr. Sawyer, who is her supervisor. Ms. Rose feels Mr. Sawyer's behavior is reprehensible, that Anna is being exploited, and that Mr. Sawyer should be dismissed immediately. Ms. Rose asks that Mr. Duncan speak to Anna Mendoza and tell her of the risks and dangers of dating Mr. Sawyer. Mr. Duncan assures Ms. Rose that he will check into the matter immediately. He tells Ms. Rose that at this point it is not appropriate for him or Ms. Rose to speak to Anna Mendoza or Mr. Sawyer about their alleged affair.

Questions for Discussion

1. What additional information would help you better understand this case?

2. How do you think Ms. Rose feels on hearing the information about the alleged affair from her trustworthy student?

3. Did Ms. Rose act appropriately in talking to her director, Mr. Duncan, about this alleged affair? Why or why not?

4. How do you think Mr. Duncan feels on hearing Ms. Rose's concerns?

5. Should Mr. Duncan verify the information that Ms. Rose has given him? If so, how can he do this?

6. If the information is found to be untrue and based on gossip, what action, if any, should Mr. Duncan take?

7. If gossip is ruled out, what is Mr. Duncan's responsibility to investigate further?

8. To what extent could Mr. Sawyer's alleged behavior be viewed as sexual harassment?

9. If the information that Ms. Rose conveyed is found to be true, who, if anyone, should Mr. Duncan inform about the situation?

10. Does it seem appropriate for faculty and administrators to do anything to break up an affair between consenting adults when they think the affair is harmful to one of the parties involved? If so, what are possible actions they could take?

11. What options does Ms. Rose have at this point? Evaluate each option.

12. What options does Mr. Duncan have in this situation? Evaluate each option.

Extending the Case

Consider the four situations presented. Then reflect on these questions: (1) How does each situation differ from or relate to this case? (2) What contributing factors come into play in each situation? and (3) What are the possible courses of action for each?

1. A Cambodian student informs the program director that a Spanish man in his class asked him to go to a gay bar with him last weekend. He says that he declined the offer politely and that the Spanish student has not repeated his invitation. The Cambodian student explains that he is uncomfortable around this Spanish classmate and asks to be transferred to another class.

2. A Thai woman informs the department chair that her male instructor offered, and has been giving her, private tutoring outside of class. One time he suggested that they go off campus to a restaurant where they could practice English in a natural setting. Reluctantly, she agreed; she did not know if the instructor's behavior was usual, and she didn't know how to politely refuse. They had dinner at an expensive restaurant where he commented on her beauty, explicitly mentioning

her breasts, lips, and other physical features. When she asked him to take her back to her residence hall, he did. She tells the director that she is uncomfortable around the teacher and in his class. She asks to transfer to another section of the same course and asks the director to tell the teacher that she does not want to meet with him again.

3. Several of the teachers at the adult school suspect that two of the students in their early twenties, one from Haiti and the other from France, are romantically involved and have moved in with each other.

4. A graduate student from Belarus works closely with her male professor and advisor on her research project. Spending long hours together, they discover that they enjoy each other's company, are physically attracted to each other, and they begin dating.

Questions for Further Reflection

1. What are the advantages and disadvantages of a program and/or institution having a policy forbidding faculty and staff to date students?

2. In what situations is it appropriate to move a student to a different class because of uncomfortable or troublesome interpersonal relationships with another student in the class? With the instructor of the class?

3. List examples of specific kinds of power that faculty have over students in class.

4. How do you think the power differential between an instructor and student impact personal relationships?

5. What do you think are appropriate actions for a faculty member to take if he or she becomes aware of each of the following situations?

   a.   a consensual relationship between two adult students

   b.   a consensual relationship between an adult student and a minor

   c.   an alleged act of sexual harassment between two adult students

   d.   a consensual relationship between an instructor and a student who is a minor

   e.   an alleged act of sexual harassment between an instructor and a student

6. What do you think are possible appropriate actions for a director to take if he or she becomes aware of the each of the following situations?

   a. a consensual relationship between two adult students

   b. a consensual relationship between an adult student and a minor

   c. an alleged act of sexual harassment between two adult students

   d. a consensual relationship between an instructor and a student who is a minor

   e. an alleged act of sexual harassment between an instructor and a student

7. What actions should a faculty member take if a student indicates that he or she has been sexually harassed on campus? Off campus? Do the actions taken depend upon the permission of the student lodging the complaint?

8. Under what circumstances does it seem appropriate for faculty to inform students of their rights and responsibilities with regard to romantic involvement and sexual harassment in academic settings? If so, how could faculty do this?

Delving Deeper

1. Using the Internet and print materials, research the legal definition of *sexual harassment* and of *consensual dating* in the United States. What constitutes sexual harassment? Give clear examples of sexual harassment and clear examples of consensual dating. How do you think these terms might be defined differently in other countries and cultures? Write about your findings and be prepared to discuss them. Document your sources appropriately.

2. Examine the website of two or three institutions for definitions of and policies on sexual harassment. For example, does the institution offer and/or require employees to attend workshops on sexual harassment? What is the reporting process for alleged acts of sexual harassment? Compare and evaluate the institutions' definitions and policies. Be prepared to share your findings in writing or orally. Document your sources.

3. It is common to find faculty members married to, or in long-term relationships with, other faculty members at the same institution. Think of your own experience as a student and reflect on a situation in which two faculty members were married or involved in a stable romantic relationship. How, if at all, did their relationship impact you and your educational experience?

4. On occasion, a faculty member and her or his student become romantically involved. List three potential risks associated with a faculty-student romantic relationship.

Resources

Coffey, M., & Grace, S. (1997). *Intercultural advising in English-language programs.* Washington, DC: NAFSA.

Kadison, R., & DiGeronimo, T. F. (2004). *College of the overwhelmed: The campus mental health crisis and what to do about it.* San Francisco, CA: Jossey-Bass.

National Center for Victims of Crime. www.ncvc.org.

U.S. Equal Employment Opportunity Commission. www.eeoc.gov/types/sexual_harassment.html.

Resolution to the Featured Case

As promised, Mr. Duncan immediately looked into the matter by talking confidentially to a manager in the Human Resources Department, someone whom he knew well and had worked with often. He learned that the institution did not have a policy against faculty or staff dating students. The human resources manager informed him that if it was a consensual affair, there was nothing that he or the institution could do. Both Anna and Mr. Sawyer were adults. They both agreed that if the situation was as Ms. Rose described it that it was troublesome and that Mr. Sawyer's actions seemed inappropriate. They also agreed that the situation could easily develop into a harmful situation.

Mr. Duncan told Ms. Rose what he had learned and that there was nothing they could do if there was a consensual affair. He reminded her that he had not been able to confirm the rumors. Ms. Rose was not pleased with the news and took her complaints about Mr. Sawyer to his supervisor.

Mr. Duncan never learned if the rumors were true, but he heard the same rumors from others on campus and suspected that Anna and Mr. Sawyer were having an affair. About six months after Mr. Duncan first heard the rumors, Mr. Sawyer was asked to leave and moved away. Anna continued to be a student at the college and eventually completed her degree.

MY THOUGHTS **on the Resolution**

Case 35 Collegiality

Sally Cassidy, a conscientious young instructor, teaches immigrants three nights a week in a local adult school. Her class is from 8:00–9:45 PM, immediately after Jerry Mason's class in the same room. Ms. Cassidy, a new instructor, and Mr. Mason, a long-time instructor at the school, know each other, but they are not personal friends. Ms. Cassidy almost always has difficulty beginning her class on time because Mr. Mason holds his class past 8:00 even though it technically ends at 7:45 PM. By the time his students leave and Ms. Cassidy's students get to their seats, 15 or more minutes of class time are lost. Additionally, Mr. Mason seldom erases the blackboards, so Ms. Cassidy has to take time to do this before she begins class.

One evening, Ms. Cassidy politely and somewhat timidly asks Mr. Mason to end class on time and to erase the blackboards before he leaves. He smiles and says, "Students arrive late and they need their full class time. I'll try to remember to erase the blackboards." Despite Ms. Cassidy's initial and subsequent requests, nothing changes. Mr. Mason continues to hold class until after 8:00, and the blackboards are seldom erased. In fact, Mr. Mason seems unsympathetic and unapologetic. Ms. Cassidy becomes more and more annoyed each night. She can't keep her students past 9:45, as some have to catch buses shortly after that. She isn't sure what to do.

Questions for Discussion

1. What additional information would help you better understand this case?

2. How might Mr. Mason view Ms. Cassidy's request?

3. How might Ms. Cassidy view Mr. Mason's behavior and response to her request?

4. How might the students in Mr. Mason's class view this situation? How might the students in Ms. Cassidy's class view the situation?

168

5. What are Ms. Cassidy's and Mr. Mason's professional obligations to their students?

6. List examples of professional courtesies involved in this case.

7. Mr. Mason is older and a long-time instructor at the school whereas Ms. Cassidy is young and a new instructor. How might gender, age, and experience influence their behaviors in this situation?

8. Does it appear that Mr. Mason and Ms. Cassidy have equal power? Explain your answer.

9. What options does Mr. Mason have in this situation? Evaluate each option.

10. What options does Ms. Cassidy have in this situation? Evaluate each option.

Extending the Case

Consider the three situations presented. Then reflect on these questions: (1) How does each situation differ from or relate to this case? (2) What contributing factors come into play in each situation? and (3) What are the possible courses of action for each?

1. An instructor with a small class always rearranges the desks and chairs in her classroom for group work, stacking unused chairs in the back of the room. The following class is a large lecture class where every chair in the room is needed. The second instructor asks the first instructor to please rearrange the furniture for a lecture setup.

2. The advanced writing teacher in an IEP has arranged for a librarian to give her class a tour of the university library. The library is a 15-minute walk from the building where the classes are held, and she fears that students will not have enough time between classes to arrive at the appointed time. She asks the grammar instructor before her class if he can let the students out five to ten minutes early so that they have time to get to the library on time. She offers to let him have time from her class on another day to make up for lost class time.

3. Two faculty members, a man and a woman, are assigned to organize an educational field trip and take their two classes together on the trip. Despite repeated requests by the female faculty member, the male faculty member never has time to meet and talk about the field trip. They talk briefly in the teachers' lounge before and after class. Every suggestion that she makes, he readily accepts. In the end, she makes all arrangements and prepares all the handouts for lessons before and after the field trip for both classes. Her colleague is affable and well-liked by students. The field trip and classwork associated with it are a big success. The supervisor compliments both faculty on a job well done after hearing favorable comments from students in both classes.

Questions for Further Reflection

1. What are some common courtesies colleagues using the same classroom can practice to make classes run smoothly and help students benefit as much as possible from instruction?

2. What liberties with regard to such issues as class start-stop time, location, and use of facilities are acceptable in the U.S. academic environment? Who needs to be informed of deviations in assigned class operations (e.g., class time, location), and when should they be informed?

3. What are some common courtesies that seem appropriate for colleagues to practice when they use the same work space?

4. What options does an instructor have for dealing with a colleague who seems not to be pulling his or her weight? Evaluate each option.

5. How important is it to like your colleagues as individuals? Is it important that ELT faculty share the same views about pedagogy and other instructional issues?

6. What are some characteristics of an ideal colleague?

7. What are some strategies for successfully working with difficult colleagues?

Delving Deeper

1. Research sources on the Internet and in print for ways of dealing with difficult people at work. Think of your own experience in working and interacting with others. What methods have you found effective for successful interactions? Make a list of advice for dealing with difficult people at work. Make a list of effective strategies and share it with others. Document your sources appropriately.

2. Achieving happiness at work is something everyone struggles with. Research Internet and print sources for reasons individuals may not be happy at work (e.g., boredom, lack of autonomy, inadequate compensation) and advice on how to improve one's satisfaction. Write about your findings and document your sources appropriately.

3. Scenes depicting frustration and trouble at work are often found in movies (e.g., *Nine to Five, North Country*) and in TV shows (e.g., *The Office, The Simpsons*). Choose a movie or TV episode. Describe the work situation and analyze the interactions of the characters. Write about your findings and share them with others.

Resources

Csikszentmihalyi, M. (1997). *Finding flow: The psychology of engagement with everyday life*. New York: Basic Books.

Dalai Lama (with Cutler, H. C.). (1998). *The art of happiness: A handbook for living*. New York: Riverhead.

————. (2003). *The art of happiness at work*. New York: Riverhead.

Internet Movie Database. www.imdb.com.

Scott, G. G. (2004). *A survival guide for working with humans: Dealing with whiners, back-stabbers, know-it-alls, and other difficult people*. New York: Amacom.

Seligman, M. P. (2006). *Learned optimism: How to change your mind and your life*. New York: Vintage.

Solomon, M. (2002) *Working with difficult people*. New York: Prentice Hall.

Resolution to the Featured Case

Ms. Cassidy decided to speak to the chair of the department about the situation concerning Mr. Mason. The chair listened sympathetically and said that she would speak to Mr. Mason. When he did, Mr. Mason was annoyed and accused Ms. Cassidy of being overly sensitive and of exaggerating the situation. He did not feel there was a problem. The department chair asked that Mr. Mason begin and end class on time and that he erase the blackboard after each class. Mr. Mason said he'd try. In fact, nothing changed.

MY THOUGHTS **on the Resolution**

Case 36 Integrity

Mr. Edwards teaches composition part-time in an IEP at a local university. He is not especially popular with the students, and they sometimes complain about him to the administrator. Mrs. Blount, the director, is sympathetic and tries to hire other people for the position, but she often cannot find anyone else on short notice. She is puzzled because Mr. Edwards' teaching evaluations are generally average or slightly higher than average.

When conducting evaluations, the instructor is contractually required to follow a set procedure. A faculty member appoints a student to take over the process and must leave the classroom while the students complete the evaluations. The student passes out the evaluation forms, collects them, seals the envelope, signs across the seal and then asks the faculty member to do the same. The student then immediately brings the envelope with the evaluations to the administrative office.

One semester, when the student comes to the office to return Mr. Edwards' evaluations, Mrs. Blount casually asks her what she thinks about the process since student evaluation of faculty may be new to non-U.S. students. The student states that she did exactly what Mr. Edwards told her to do. She also mentions that Mr. Edwards told the class how important it is for him to get good evaluations in order to keep his job and that he urged them to rate him highly.

Questions for Discussion

1. What additional information would help you better understand this case?

2. How do you think students feel about evaluating faculty?

3. How do you think the teacher-student relationship and the educational system in students' home countries influence their reactions to the process?

4. How can faculty assist students who are not familiar with the process of evaluating faculty without biasing their responses?

173

5. What can administrators do to help ensure that evaluations are conducted fairly?

6. What options does Mrs. Blount have in this situation? Evaluate each option.

Extending the Case

Consider the three situations presented. Then reflect on these questions: (1) How does each situation differ from or relate to this case? (2) What contributing factors come into play in each situation? and (3) What are the possible courses of action for each party involved?

1. A young woman applies for a teaching position at a local community college where the basic requirement for the position is the M.A. degree in TESOL. She has completed all of the courses for the degree at a nearby university but has not finished her thesis. However, her prospectus has been approved, and thus she feels that she can safely claim that she has earned the degree and makes that claim on her resume. She is a gregarious individual and is one of the finalists for the position. In the interview she discusses her thesis as though it were complete. The search committee is very impressed with her and recommends her for the position.

2. Several part-time instructors at an IEP decide to supplement their income by tutoring students outside of class. They distribute flyers and post announcements offering their services at an hourly rate. Several students in their own classes contact them and ask to be tutored, especially with essays and class projects. The students agree to pay the posted hourly fee.

3. A new part-time faculty member at a university shares with colleagues her concerns about whether she will be rehired in future semesters and the hope that perhaps she will eventually be offered a full-time position. Her full-time and part-time colleagues who have been teaching at the institution for years advise her to grade easy, giving students As and Bs so that her student evaluations will be high. They tell her that without high ratings from students, she will not be rehired.

Questions for Further Reflection

1. Define integrity within the academic context, specifically as the issue relates to faculty. List some issues that might involve integrity, such as turning in grades on time and maintaining regularly scheduled office hours. Be specific.

2. There is often a fine line between portraying oneself in a favorable light on a resume or in an interview and stretching the truth. Give examples of each.

3. What consequences or follow-up actions, if any, seem appropriate for each of the examples you list in Question 2 if the potential employer discovers an irregularity in information provided by the applicant? Explain your answers.

4. Search committees often consist of faculty who are already very busy. What are some of the basic pieces of information search committees need to verify for each candidate considered?

5. If faculty tutor students outside of class, what guidelines or understandings (e.g., about payment, content) should be in place between the instructor and the students?

6. What are the advantages and disadvantages of ESL faculty having different student evaluation forms from other faculty (e.g., science, math, history, business) at an institution? What kinds of information and questions might be specifically relevant to ESL faculty on such forms?

7. What are the advantages and disadvantages of faculty developing their own questionnaires or course evaluations in order to get feedback from students about textbooks, activities, and instructional materials?

8. If faculty develop their own surveys about their classes to help them improve their teaching, when should such surveys be conducted (e.g., early in the semester, mid-semester, near the end of the semester)? How might surveys differ in terms of purpose and types of questions at different times in the session/semester? Give some examples.

9. How can administrators and program directors help ensure that faculty evaluations are conducted professionally?

Delving Deeper

1. In education, two broad types of faculty evaluation methods are typically discussed: formative and summative. Search for information in print materials or on the Internet to help you define each, explain how they differ, and give an example of a question that might be found on each. Document your sources.

2. Issues of faculty integrity range from extremely serious, such as falsifying research results, to seemingly minor transgressions, such as failing to be available during posted office hours. List four or five breaches of faculty academic integrity. Which are the most serious? Which are the least important? With others, discuss the possible consequences of each item on your list.

Resources

Kennedy, D. (1997). *Academic duty.* Cambridge, MA: Harvard University Press.

Pennington, M. C., & Young, A. L. (1991). Procedures and instruments for faculty evaluation in ESL. In M. Pennington (Ed.). *Building better English language programs: Perspectives on evaluation in ESL* (pp. 191–205). Washington, DC: NAFSA.

Resolution to the Featured Case

Mrs. Blount spoke to Mr. Edwards about his evaluations, as she did with all faculty. Without specifically accusing him of wrongdoing, she went over the need to avoid biasing the students' responses with casual comments about the importance of getting high ratings. She resolved to try harder to find a replacement for Mr. Edwards.

MY THOUGHTS on the Resolution

Case 37 Linguistic Competence

Late one afternoon after classes end, two Korean students come to the IEP office to speak to the director, Ms. Fielding. This is the second week of the first term for the intermediate-level men. After they are seated in Ms. Fielding's office, the older man states that they believe that their oral communication instructor, Ms. Hahn, is not good because she is Korean and her pronunciation is not like a native English speaker's. The other man adds that Ms. Hahn is a nice teacher, but they want a native speaker. They fear that they cannot learn how to speak well in her class and so request to move to another section and thus have a different instructor for their oral communication class. Ms. Fielding listens politely, allowing them plenty of time to state their arguments.

Ms. Hahn has an advanced degree in TESOL from a U.S. university, has lived in the United States for many years, and is fluent in English, with no trace of a foreign accent. Additionally, she is multilingual, and fluent in Korean and Chinese as well as in English. Ms. Fielding has complete confidence in Ms. Hahn as a teacher and is unsure about how to respond to the students' request.

Questions for Discussion

1. What additional information would help you better understand this case?

2. What do you think are the students' perceptions of Ms. Hahn? What do their perceptions seem to be based on?

3. How do you think Ms. Fielding feels on hearing the students' request and arguments?

4. What are Ms. Fielding's responsibilities to Ms. Hahn when speaking to these students? In general, what is an administrator's responsibilities to faculty members when students make complaints about them?

178

5. What are Ms. Fielding's responsibilities to these two students and all the program students?

6. What are the advantages and disadvantages of Ms. Fielding informing Ms. Hahn of the students' request and their arguments?

7. What options does Ms. Fielding have for dealing with their request? Evaluate each option.

Extending the Case

Consider the three situations presented. Then reflect on these questions: (1) How does each situation differ from or relate to this case? (2) What contributing factors come into play in each situation? and (3) What are the possible courses of action for each?

1. A recent graduate is hired at the last minute to teach a job skills preparation class for newly arrived Asians, mainly Chinese, for a community-based organization. Originally from Taiwan, the new hire majored in English and had good grades. However, she is still not completely fluent in English. One evening, her supervisor overhears the new instructor having her students repeat ungrammatical sentences. Though the supervisor knew that the new hire's English was still somewhat weak, the supervisor is disappointed to learn that she seems to lack the skills for teaching the low-level class. The supervisor is annoyed with herself for not having had the time to interview the new instructor in more depth or to check her references before hiring her.

2. A new international graduate student from India in the M.A. TESOL program at a large university begins looking for work on campus as soon as she arrives. She learns that some of her fellow students from the U.S. and Canada have teaching assistantships in the IEP on campus, so she decides to apply for a TA position. When she submits her resume and asks for an interview with the director, the program assistant informs her that generally TAs are native English speakers. She is advised to apply for a teaching assistantship in the Modern Language Department. The student explains that she is from India, received her education in English, and grew up speaking English as well as several other languages.

3. The director of a small IEP housed in a downtown metropolitan area is pleased that enrollment is larger than expected for the upcoming session. He needs another teacher immediately, however, and is unsure about where to find one. In searching through resumes he has recently received, he decides to call and set up interviews with two applicants. Both applicants have appropriate advanced degrees. After the interviews, the director thinks that both would do an okay job but likes one candidate better because his experience more directly matches the requirements of the position and his references are better than the other candidate's. However, he has a concern about his preferred candidate's speech patterns because, unlike the other candidate, his preferred candidate has a heavy regional accent; during the interview, he used slang and other expressions the director considered inappropriate. The director isn't sure which candidate to hire.

Questions for Further Reflection

1. What does it mean to be a native English speaker (NES)?

2. What does it mean to be a non-native English speaker (NNES)?

3. How important is pronunciation in the evaluation of a job applicant for a teaching position (e.g., does an instructor need to sound like a native speaker)? How important is grammatical accuracy?

4. What barriers do NNES instructors typically face?

5. What advantages do NNES professionals bring to the ESL classroom?

6. How can colleagues, supervisors, and NNES professionals handle student criticism that NNES instructors are not native speakers of English and thus not as qualified as NES instructors?

7. How can NNES and NES colleagues support each other?

8. What are the advantages of NES and NNES professionals collaborating on courses and/or projects? On teacher development projects?

9. What are some ways a director or supervisor can verify an applicant's linguistic competence to teach?

10. What actions can a director take if he or she learns that an instructor's English ability is weak? What can a director do to support the employee and ensure the quality of instruction?

Delving Deeper

1. Research Internet and print sources for the definitions and explanations of the phrases (a) *idealization of the native speaker,* and (b) *the native speaker fallacy* as they pertain to the field of ELT. Is the distinction between native speakers and non–native English speakers a valid one in general? Is it a valid distinction in terms of educators who teach English? Write about these issues and be prepared to share your ideas with others. Document your sources appropriately.

2. The goal of the traditional model for teaching English pronunciation has been to have speakers sound like native speakers. More recently, researchers have argued that the goal should be to help non-native speakers be intelligible and comprehensible. What arguments can be made for each model? Does the appropriateness of each model depend upon the context and situation of the NNES? Find sources to support both arguments. How might classroom pedagogy differ for each model? If you are in a group setting, you may wish to frame the discussion as a debate, with individuals taking different positions.

Resources

Braine, G. (Ed.). (1999). *Non-native educators in English language teaching.* Mahwah, NJ: Lawrence Erlbaum.

Canagarajah, A. S. (1999). Interrogating the "native speaker fallacy": Non-linguistic roots, non-pedagogical results. In G. Braine (Ed.), *Non-native educators in English language teaching* (pp. 77–92). Mahwah, NJ: Lawrence Erlbaum.

Crystal, D. (1997). *English as a global language.* New York: Cambridge University Press.

Jenkins, J. (2000). *The phonology of English as an international language.* New York: Oxford University Press.

Kamhi-Stein, L. D. (Theme Section Ed.). (2001). Nonnative English-speaking professionals. *CATESOL Journal, 13*(1), 47–160.

Kramsch, C. (1997). The privilege of the nonnative speaker. *PMLA, 112,* 359–369.

Levis, J. M. (Ed.). (2005). Pronunciation teaching [Special issue]. *TESOL Quarterly, 39*(3), 365–572.

Nayar, P .B. (1994, April). Whose English is it? *TESL-EJ, 1*(1). www-writing. berkeley.edu/TESL-EJ/ej01/f.1.html.

Non-Native English Speakers in TESOL Interest Section: The Official Website. http://nnest.asu.edu/.

Widdowson, H. G. (1994). The ownership of English. *TESOL Quarterly, 28*, 377–389.

Resolution to the Featured Case

After listening carefully to the Korean men and asking a few questions, Ms. Fielding explained that Ms. Hahn was an excellent teacher with extensive experience, an advanced degree, and no trace of a foreign accent. Ms. Fielding expressed her complete confidence in Ms. Hahn and assured the students that Ms. Hahn was very attentive to individual student needs and that they would learn much in her class. Ms. Fielding closed by thanking the students for coming to her to express their concerns and telling them that they were welcome to come speak to her at any time.

After the students left, Ms. Fielding decided that there was no need to tell Ms. Hahn about the students' concerns. The students did not speak to Ms. Fielding about this matter again.

MY THOUGHTS on the Resolution

Case 38 Instructor Effectiveness

Mabinty Kargbo, a woman from the Ivory Coast, visits the program director, Mr. Ferrara, to complain about her writing instructor, Ms. Pritchard, whom she says is teaching very little in her writing class. When questioned, she says that they have written two essays in six weeks, submitting two drafts of each. They spend much of the class time discussing readings and doing sentence-level grammar exercises. Ms. Pritchard provides little feedback on papers. Mabinty indicates that Mrs. Pritchard writes few comments and marks none of the grammatical errors. She shows the director a first draft of an essay on which Ms. Pritchard wrote two sentences only: "Check your grammar," and "Write more." She indicates that on the final draft, Ms. Pritchard writes only the grade, giving no suggestions for improvement nor comments on strengths and weaknesses of the essay. She says that she generally gets a B or B+. She stresses that her complaint is not about her grade but about the fact that she doesn't think that she is learning much in the class.

Questions for Discussion

1. What additional information would help you better understand this case?

2. How do you think Mabinty feels about speaking to Mr. Ferrara?

3. How do you think Mr. Ferrara feels on hearing Mabinty's concerns?

4. What do you think are some reasons for Ms. Pritchard's method of commenting on and correcting essays?

5. Assuming that the limited information that you have about Ms. Pritchard's class is true, does Mabinty's complaint seem legitimate? Explain your answer.

6. What options does Mr. Ferrara have in responding to Mabinty during their conversation? Evaluate each option.

7. What possible actions can Mr. Ferrara take following this meeting? Evaluate each possiblity.

Extending the Case

Consider the three situations presented. Then reflect on these questions: (1) How does each situation differ from or relate to this case? (2) What contributing factors come into play in each situation? and (3) What are the possible courses of action for each?

1. The 30 students in an intermediate reading class have a wide range of English abilities. The assigned text is at the appropriate level for the majority of students, but there are two students for whom the book is not challenging and five for whom the book is too difficult. Wanting to be sure that all students master the material, the instructor decides to teach to the lowest-performing students. Thus, she reviews and tests vocabulary most students know, and she carefully goes over each page in each lesson until she feels all the students know the material. The majority of students find the class very slow and uninteresting.

2. A newly hired director reviews the credentials and teaching evaluations of the present faculty. He discovers that two faculty members who have been teaching for many years have only bachelor degrees, one in politics and the other in business. He has met both of them and they each seem pleasant and responsible. They are both native speakers of English and have traveled abroad, one having lived in Japan for a year. He finds that one's teaching evaluations are below average, whereas the other one's are average.

3. One semester a popular instructor is assigned an advanced grammar class, which he has never taught before. He regularly spends time chatting with students outside of class, often joining groups for lunch or coffee. In class, he relies heavily on the textbook, reading the grammatical explanations to the students and asking them to follow along. He then does the exercises in the book as class exercises and assigns additional exercises from the book as homework. Homework is generally checked in class. If asked for a grammatical explanation of a specific point, he generally rereads the rules or charts in the book or refers students to the relevant pages. Students like him, but they wonder if he knows the subject.

Questions for Further Reflection

1. List four to six qualities that make a good ESOL instructor. Which of these qualities do the featured case and the three extensions highlight? Which of these qualities are lacking in the featured case and extensions? Explain your answers.

2. How does an instructor's feeling of being a professional affect his or her teaching? How does being treated as a professional affect one's teaching?

3. Teaching has been called a science and an art. What aspects of teaching seem to fit into each category? Explain your answer.

4. What does it mean for an instructor to be prepared for class? Be specific.

5. What are some reasons instructors come to class unprepared? Which reasons would be considered legitimate and which ones would not?

6. List two or three negative consequences of following a lesson plan too closely.

7. What strategies can an instructor use to prepare for a course he or she has never taught before? Before beginning the class? During the session when she is teaching the class?

8. Instructors have many basic responsibilities to their students, such as holding class, arriving to class on time, being prepared, and using the assigned textbook. List three to five other responsibilities or obligations that instructors have to students in their classes. You may wish to draw on your own experiences as a student or as an instructor. Explain your answers.

9. What are two or three factors that an instructor should consider when setting the pace of a particular lesson or class period? Of a course?

10. How do you respond to the assertion that anyone who is a native speaker of English can teach it?

Delving Deeper

1. Think of an inspiring instructor that you have had. What qualities did he or she possess? What talents? Try to think of details about how this individual went about the daily tasks of being an excellent instructor and creating a stimulating learning environment for students. Write about this person and your experiences. Be ready to share them orally.

2. Teaching writing is challenging, and evaluating written work is difficult and often time consuming. Using the Internet and print resources, define and explain each of the following types of testing or assessment for writing: (a) holistic grading, (b) portfolio evaluation, and (c) the use of rubrics. List the advantages and disadvantages of each for evaluating writing in a course (not on an institutional level). Are there other ways to evaluate students' writing ability? Write about your findings and share them with others. Document your sources appropriately.

3. Teaching mixed-level classes is a challenge and one of the most common frustrations for new instructors. The reality is that mixed-level classes are inevitable even with well-devised placement testing procedures. Identify a class (e.g., conversation, writing, grammar) and a designated proficiency level (e.g., basic, intermediate, high-intermediate, advanced). Devise three to four activities for this class and level that could be used with students of mixed abilities. You may wish to get ideas from the Internet or print materials. Write about the activities and be prepared to explain them to others. Document your sources.

Resources

Brown, H. D. (2001). How to plan a lesson. In H. D. Brown, *Teaching by principles: An integrative approach to language pedagogy* (2nd ed.), pp. 149–163. White Plains, NY: Pearson.

Burt, M. K., & Kiparsky, C. (1972). *The gooficon: A repair manual for English.* Rowley, MA: Newbury House.

Casanave, C. P. (2004). *Controversies in second language writing: Dilemmas and decisions in research and instruction.* Ann Arbor: University of Michigan Press.

Ferris, D. R. (1997). The influence of teacher commentary on student revision. *TESOL Quarterly, 31,* 315–339.

———. (2002). *Treatment of error in second language student writing.* Ann Arbor: University of Michigan Press.

Leki, I. (1992). *Understanding ESL writers: A guide for teachers.* Portsmouth, NH: Boynton/Cook-Heinemann.

Pasternak, M., & Bailey, K. (2004). Preparing nonnative and native English-speaking teachers: Issues of professionalism and proficiency. In L.D. Kamhi-Stein (Ed.), *Learning and teaching from experience: Perspectives on nonnative English-speaking professionals* (pp. 155-175). Ann Arbor: University of Michigan Press.

Simpson, D. J., Jackson, M. J. B., Aycock, J. C. (2005). *John Dewey and the art of teaching: Toward reflective and imaginative practice.* Thousand Oaks, CA: Sage.

Snow, M.A., Kamhi-Stein, L.D., & Brinton, D.M. (2006). Teacher training for English as a lingua franca. *Annual Review of Applied Linguistics, 26,* 261–281.

Resolution to the Featured Case

Mr. Ferrara spoke to Ms. Pritchard about her writing class, eliciting information about how the class was going. Mr. Ferrara told Ms. Pritchard about a student speaking to him, expressing the desire for more writing assignments and more feedback on papers. Ms. Pritchard became defensive, explaining that she worked hard and that grading essays took a lot of time. She said that she simply didn't have time to correct errors or provide many comments on papers because she had 20 students in the class. She also indicated that students had written two essays, each with two drafts during the session. Mr. Ferrara suggested ways to give students more writing and make the grading load more manageable for Ms. Pritchard. Getting little response from Ms. Pritchard, Mr. Ferrara finally reminded her of the required number of essays for the class, which were outlined in the learning objectives for the course, and he urged her to provide students with more feedback on their papers.

MY THOUGHTS **on the Resolution**

Case 39
Students as Research Subjects

Jeanne Kronopolis is working on her doctorate and decides to undertake a qualitative case study of a community college ESL program in her area. She has designed her research questions and outlined a good methodology, including interviews with selected students, instructors, and supervisors. She also plans to examine textbooks and observe several classes, taking copious field notes in order to provide a thick description and videotaping classes and then analyzing each tape. After developing her research proposal and obtaining clearance from her committee and the Protection of Human Subjects Committee at her home institution, she drives to the community college to ask the department chair, Dr. Barnes, for permission to conduct her study at his campus. She obtained his name from her advisor. She assures Dr. Barnes that she plans to follow the procedures required by her university for the protection of human subjects. He denies her request; however, he is most apologetic. Dr. Barnes explains that he cannot allow her to undertake her study in the community college classes as she has outlined it. He is especially concerned about the videotaping segment. Dr. Barnes explains that the classes at his college have undocumented students who simply leave class at the sight of a video camera and then sometimes never return. He is adamant about making the classes a comfortable, safe place for all students.

Questions for Discussion

1. What additional information would help you better understand this case?

2. How do you think Jeanne feels about Dr. Barnes' response to her request?

3. How could Jeanne have done things differently to avoid being denied access to the classes?

4. What responsibility does Dr. Barnes have to safeguard the students in his classes?

5. To what extent, if any, do you feel that the events of 9/11 and the current atmosphere in the U.S. towards immigrants, documented and undocumented, influenced Dr. Barnes' decision?

6. What are some ways Dr. Barnes could assist Jeanne Kronopolis with her research? Is he obligated to do so?

Extending the Case

Consider the four situations presented. Then reflect on these questions: (1) How does each situation differ from or relate to this case? (2) What contributing factors come into play in each situation? and (3) What are the possible courses of action for each?

1. A doctoral-level graduate student in psychology is conducting research on the issue of homesickness. He is trying to determine to what extent length of time away from home is a factor in feeling homesick and feels that the students in the IEP are perfect subjects for his work. He finds out the name of the instructor in the advanced writing class and catches her on her way to her morning class. He walks with her to class and tells her he needs to administer a short questionnaire to her students that morning. He needs about twenty minutes of class time. The instructor refuses his request.

2. An instructor and his colleague are conducting research on how well international students know what kinds of health and safety precautions are advisable in the city where they are studying. The two faculty members administer a questionnaire, which has been approved by the Human Subjects Board of the university. Students are advised in writing of the research project and all sign that they are willing to participate. A couple of the questions are on the topic of safe sex. After class, a student complains to the instructor about the content of the questionnaire.

3. An M.A. TESOL student emails the director of the local adult school asking if she can interview eight to ten Spanish-speaking students about their English-learning experiences. The student indicates that the research is for one of her classes. She attaches a set of draft interview questions that the director finds poorly written and unfocused.

4. The director of a university-based IEP approves the research project of a doctoral student at the same university. The director emails
the faculty explaining the research and its potential benefits to the
program. He requests all of the faculty members to administer the
questionnaire on the same day because the doctoral student needs to
be certain that all of the students complete the questionnaire as close
to the same time as possible. Two faculty members email back and
decline to administer the questionnaire saying they cannot sacrifice
the class time because they have too much material to cover.

Questions for Further Reflection

1. To what extent is an instructor obliged to allow research projects on
students in his or her classes?

2. What are some guidelines an instructor or program could use to
evaluate proposed research projects involving ESL students?

3. What are some reasonable and appropriate rules of etiquette for
researchers to follow in requesting permission to conduct research?

4. How much information about the type of questions in a research
study should researchers give prospective participants?

5. To what extent should researchers consider the cultural mores of
students when designing and developing research instruments?

6. Are there ways researchers can develop culturally sensitive instruments?
Give some examples.

7. What kinds of research projects can benefit ESL students, individual
classes, and programs? What are some benefits of these projects?

Delving Deeper

1. Locate a sample statement or guidelines regarding the protection of human subjects for research purposes. Your own institution undoubtedly has one, or you may wish to check for information on the Internet. If international or immigrant students are going to participate in a research project, what parts of such a policy need to be explained to them (e.g., signed permission statements)? Select two or three issues from the protocol and write about how you would explain them to an ESL class.

2. Find two research studies involving human subjects in professional journals such as the *TESOL Quarterly*. Identify any statements concerning the protection of human subjects. Compare the statements from the two studies. Given that researchers generally devote little space to explaining their procedures in this area, what questions about the process of the studies arise in your mind? What additional information might be useful about their procedures? Summarize your findings and your insights concerning these research articles.

Resources

Hafernik, J. J., & Messerschmitt, D. S. (1994). Fostering cooperation between intensive English programs and teacher education programs. *CATESOL Journal, 7*(2), 103–111.

Resolution to the Featured Case

Jeanne Kronopolis was disappointed in Dr. Barnes' response but understood his concerns. She first attempted to find a different setting for her research. Unable to do so, she modified her proposal and returned to request permission from Dr. Barnes to conduct her study at the community college. With her modifications—eliminating the videotaping of classes—he agreed to her conducting the research in the college classes. Her project was delayed by a year, but she finally graduated.

MY THOUGHTS on the Resolution

Case 40

Job Security and Support at Work

Mrs. Bell has an M. A. TESOL degree from a respected university. She also has Peace Corps experience. Ten years ago, when she moved to her current location, she applied for a teaching position in the community college district. The district hired her, part time, for a night class. Because she regularly received positive student evaluations, she gradually became a senior adjunct faculty member with preferences regarding her teaching schedule and annual raises. She would like to be a full-time instructor but is not and, thus, has only limited medical benefits. Last semester, she was scheduled to teach a writing class in the morning. After several weeks preparing her syllabus and the assignments, she met the class on the first day, but only five students enrolled. The students were moved to another section, which had only nine students and was taught by someone with more seniority than Mrs. Bell. Mrs. Bell's class was cancelled. At such a late date, there were no other classes for the department chair to assign to Mrs. Bell. Fortunately, her afternoon class had 12 students, so she had one class for the semester, but half the pay she had anticipated.

Questions for Discussion

1. What additional information would help you better understand this case?

2. How do you think Mrs. Bell feels in this situation?

3. How do you think the chair of the department feels when she has to cancel one of Mrs. Bell's classes?

4. What options does the chair of the department have before cancelling the class? After deciding to cancel the class?

5. What options does Mrs. Bell have once the class is cancelled? Evaluate each option.

6. What can the department head do, if anything, to avoid such situations in the future? To ameliorate such situations in the future?

Extending the Case

Consider the three situations presented. Then reflect on these questions: (1) How does each situation differ from or relate to this case? (2) What contributing factors come into play in each situation? and (3) What are the possible courses of action for each?

1. Three faculty members at an IEP submit papers to a professional conference in another state. All three papers are accepted. Two of the faculty members are part-timers who have been with the institute for several years. One would like a full-time appointment, but no university line is open. The other wishes to remain a part-timer so that she can continue to work at her home business in jewelry design. The third is a full-time faculty member who has been with the university for several years. He would like to get a promotion to the next rank and must present at professional conferences and publish in refereed journals to be eligible. He has delivered a paper at the conference for three consecutive years and received funding from the institute to cover most of his expenses. Again this year, with considerable difficulty, the director of the institute has set aside some funds for professional travel, but the amount is not nearly enough to cover all three faculty members. Nevertheless, all three request funding for the conference.

2. A new instructor at a local adult school purchases four new books for her professional library, a set of miniature grocery products for several lessons on food, and a box of flashcards on irregular verbs. She saves her receipts and sends an itemized sheet with her receipts attached to her administrator, asking for reimbursement. Her request is denied.

3. After the session has begun, a part-time faculty member learns that she is expected to help proctor program-wide tests and to accompany the students on a field trip at least one weekend, with no additional compensation. Fortunately, the weekend assignment does not conflict with her schedule, but the test proctoring causes a problem. Tests are given in the afternoon, and the instructor has a part-time position at another institution in the afternoon.

Questions for Further Reflection

1. What are some common features of adjunct or part-time teaching positions? Begin by listing the characteristics of Mrs. Bell's situation.

2. How is the typical situation of ESL part-time faculty similar to and/or different from faculty in other disciplines?

3. Individuals within the profession have argued that ESL faculty and students are marginalized and often not perceived as equivalent to other faculty. What support might be used to make this argument? What are some reasons this argument may be true?

4. Why do you think it may be difficult for academic institutions to predict enrollment in courses and maintain enrollment stability? List several reasons, then think about different settings (e.g., adult schools, public institutions, private institutions attracting primarily international students). Do the same reasons apply to all institutions?

5. List ways that programs and administrators can promote professional development for faculty. Next to each item on your list, indicate if additional funding is required and if a small amount or large amount of funding is needed.

6. Funding for faculty development varies according to the teaching context and institution. What are some ways for programs and faculty to obtain such funding?

7. Make a list of duties outside teaching that faculty might be expected to do (e.g., hold weekly office hours, attend meetings, advise students). For each listed duty, indicate if you feel this is a reasonable expectation for part-time faculty. Explain your opinions.

8. What types of practical information do new part-time faculty need regarding working conditions?

9. Administrators are often constrained in what they can do to alter working conditions for part-time faculty. List ways that part-time faculty could work to improve their working conditions, and indicate the kinds of administrative constraints that might exist.

10. What are some ways for faculty and administrators to work together for better working conditions for all faculty within the profession?

Delving Deeper

1. Interview a part-time faculty member in the ESL profession. Before doing so, make a list of questions, focusing on work responsibilities and conditions. Find out what duties he or she is expected to perform outside of class. What benefits, if any, are available? How stable is the instructor's position from term to term? Is the instructor satisfied with his or her working arrangement? Write about the findings of your interview and share them with others.

2. Find out what TESOL has done and is doing regarding working conditions in the field. Focus on TESOL advocacy efforts in this area. Go to your local and/or state TESOL affiliate website to see if it has position statements or advocacy efforts regarding working conditions. Write a summary of your findings. Then speculate about what else might be done to improve working conditions and support in the field.

3. Check on the Internet to find two or three employment opportunities in the U.S. or abroad that you might be interested in. Pay particular attention to the issues of compensation and benefits as well as physical working conditions such as office space and instructional facilities. Write a description of each position and explain why it interests you.

Resources

Dave's ESL Café. www.eslcafe.com.

Edge, J. (2002). *Continuing cooperative development: A discourse framework for individuals as colleagues.* Ann Arbor: University of Michigan Press.

Randall, M., & Thornton, B. (2001). *Advising and supporting teachers.* New York: Cambridge University Press.

Soppelsa, E. F. (1997). Empowerment of faculty. In M. A. Christison & F. L. Stoller (Eds.), *A handbook for language program administrators* (pp. 123–141). Burlingame, CA: Alta Book Center Publishing.

TESOL: Teachers of English to Speakers of Other Languages. www.tesol.org/s_tesol/index.asp.

Vandrick S., Hafernik, J. J., & Messerschmitt, D. S. (1994). Outsiders in academe: Women ESL faculty and their students. *Journal of Intensive English Studies, 8,* 37–55.

Resolution to the Featured Case

Mrs. Bell was disappointed that she had only one class at the community college but realized that her having two classes was contingent upon there being sufficient enrollment. Her chair suggested that she sign up to substitute throughout the district as a way to earn additional income. Mrs. Bell followed this advice and in subsequent semesters continued to teach at the community college. She repeatedly applied for the few full-time positions that became available but remained a part-time faculty member.

MY THOUGHTS **on the Resolution**